# Making the Most of Life

# Making the Most of Life

By

Charles C. Ryrie

**MOODY PRESS**
CHICAGO

Formerly entitled *Patterns for Christian Youth*

©1966 by
THE MOODY BIBLE INSTITUTE
OF CHICAGO

ISBN: 0-8024-5147-0

Printed in the United States of America

# CONTENTS

5

## It's not easy

for a Christian young person to live the Christian life today. Neither was it in New Testament times. The government was corrupt (Matt 28:14), sin was rampant and open (Rom 1:24-32), homes were not always godly (1 Cor 7:14), and many believers were slaves (Eph 6:5).

Yet God expects believers, young and old, then and now, to live godly lives. So the New Testament principles must be as workable today as they were then.

Here are some of those principles to help keep young people especially on the right track. Originally presented to a group of young people, I hope they will help you!

# 1

## *Sowing and Reaping*

TO BEGIN WITH, let's consider a fundamental law of life: "Be not deceived; God is not mocked: for whatsoever a man soweth, that shall he also reap" (Gal 6:7).

This is a law that operates in many areas of life. It is a law of nature. Whatsoever a man sows, that shall he also reap. If you sow tomatoes, you don't reap corn. You harvest tomatoes.

It is a law that governs your physical life. If you sow bad habits of eating and sleeping, you reap sickness. If you sow good ones, you reap health.

It is also a law that affects material things like the matter of giving. As a matter of fact, Paul employs the law in this very way in 2 Corinthians 9:6. In that passage he writes about being stingy or being generous, and he declares: "He which soweth sparingly shall reap also sparingly; and he which soweth bountifully shall reap also bountifully." The man who is generous finds that people are generous to him; and conversely, the stingy man reaps stinginess.

It was probably this matter of giving that brought the law to Paul's mind, for he had just been writing about supporting God's servants in Galatians 6:6. But the mention of the

9

law in Galatians 6:7 applies more to the spiritual realm than anything else. Whatever a man sows spiritually he will reap spiritually. This is further explained in verse 8 by reminding us that sowing to the flesh reaps corruption while sowing to the spirit reaps life everlasting. The law applies to many realms, but it is its outworking in this spiritual realm that I want you to think about particularly.

There are just two things you need to remember about this law.

The first is this: *It is a certain law.*

It's like gravity. It works regardless of what you think about it or whether you want it to or whether you even know about it. It is a certain law, and it will work either for ill or for good. I want to illustrate both aspects of its working—sowing to the flesh and reaping corruption, and sowing to the Spirit and reaping life.

Do you remember why the children of Israel were sent into captivity in Babylon? If you do, you're better than most Israelites, for most of them couldn't remember at all. You know it was because of idolatry and because they had neglected to keep the sabbatical year for the land for 490 years. God had commanded that every seventh year the land should lie idle, and for 490 years that wasn't done. Instead, the land was planted and the crops harvested like any other year. For 490 years the Israelites had sown to the flesh, wanting more crops, not willing to trust God to meet their needs that seventh year when the land was idle, and until the harvest of the eighth year.

Now, 490 years is a long time. Have you ever met someone whose ancestors came over on the *Mayflower*? Well, if you have, you know that such people usually boast about it. But can you imagine the kind of braggart who could be sure that his ancestors came over with Columbus? But Columbus discovered America about 490 years ago.

In 490 years a lot is forgotten, but not by God. All that time while the Israelites were going their usual way, God was keeping accounts. You know, at the beginning of each school year I'm always very glad and very sad. I am very glad to see old friends return and to meet new ones, but very sad when I realize that, if the flesh has its usual way, some students will not be in school at the beginning of next semester or next year. Some will sow fun and reap F's. Some will sow impatience and reap immaturity. Some will sow an early marriage and reap the wrong partner. Some will leave or be asked to leave. And even though you will have blessing in later life, you will never know what you missed by not sticking to the Lord's will. "Whatsoever a man soweth, that shall he also reap."

But the law works the other way too.

One of those taken into Babylonian captivity was Daniel. Now Daniel was a young teenager who could not have missed more than two of those sabbatical years owed to God. Nevertheless, he had to pay for the sins of his ancestors. But he also reaped the godly habits which his pious parents had evidently sown in his life. Our first glimpse of this boy separated from home, family, and country shows him unwilling to contaminate himself and break the Law of Moses by eating the meat of the king of Babylon. Where did he learn about the Law? How did he acquire such high principles? Apparently from godly training in his early youth. Furthermore, we see him carrying out his decision not to defile himself in a most tactful, courteous, and yet clever manner with those over him.

11

Later in his life when the threat of being thrown to the lions hung over his head, we see Daniel faithfully sowing his regular three-times-a-day prayer time with his Lord. And he reaped the protecting hand of God in the den of lions.

I hope one of the resolutions you have made for your life is to have a regular devotional time with the Lord. It is better to spend a regular though short time every day than a longer time once a week. And if you sow regular prayer now, when exam week comes, you will not crowd prayer out of your schedule. But if you do not begin now, then when the pressure is on, you will sow to the flesh and reap corruption of the flesh. It is a certain law, and it all begins to operate this week, not next.

The second thing I want you to remember about this law is this: *It is a contagious law.*

It is not a law that operates in a vacuum. I have already pointed out that the Israelites who went into captivity were not solely or entirely responsible for the failure of their ancestors to keep all those seventy sabbatical years. But what is sown often affects other people.

Look at Abraham. God promised him a child. When no child was miraculously born to his wife, Sarah, Abraham took matters into his own hands and produced his heir with Hagar by means of the flesh. Out of that union came Ishmael. A short time later Ishmael was cast out of his home, and intense hatred resulted between Sarah and Hagar. Later Ishmael married and had twelve sons and one daughter. That daughter married Esau, and from that union came the Edomites, who are the ancestors of the present-day Arabs. And you know of the conflict between the Arabs, the descendants of Abraham and Hagar, and the Jews, the descendants of Abraham and Sarah. One of the major trouble spots in our world today originated from a single act of the flesh.

You say it doesn't make any difference what you do? You say it is nobody's business but your own? You say it is your life, your body, your time, your affair. It is, but just remember that you are not a hermit living in a monastery. Not only will you reap what you sow, but what you sow and reap will affect others as well.

In a school there are always a few people who are leaders in folly. Also, they usually push themselves forward. I know also that there are many who do not approve of the foolishness of these people. Push yourselves forward, too, will you? Exert your influence for good, because if you by your positive and aggressive example sow righteousness, stability, and maturity, they will catch on. Not only will you reap more righteousness, stability, and maturity in your own life, but these things will be contagious. And would it not please the Lord to have students who have "caught" righteousness, stability, and maturity?

What you sow affects others. One of the most striking examples of this came to me once in a letter. It shows how infectiously beneficial the testimony of one student at work has been for his entire school. The letter came from a personnel manager of one of the offices in which he worked. It says:

"So often compliments are made, but never to the right person. It is with this in mind that I relate the following to you.

"Last night my next door neighbor, who works at another place, remarked that he had a man working with him who also worked part-time for my firm. It turned out to be ———, one of your students. My neighbor commented on what a fine man he was, and I agreed. Initiative, industry, reliability—he has them all.

"The main point I want to make is, however, that my neighbor said he had a lot of your students working at his company and they are all good. In fact, he said, 'I've never had a bad one! And that's the only school I can say that for.'

"He added that his personnel manager always goes to your school first when seeking part-time help for his organization."

Many more students will reap part-time jobs with that company because of the good testimony other students sowed. And while you are reaping, remember that you are also sowing for next year's student body.

What you reap at the end of a school year depends entirely on what you sow during the year. This is true of grades, friends, character, maturity, and your entire Christian growth. Whatsoever you sow, that shall you reap. The law is certain, and the effects are contagious.

# 2

## *How to Be a Good Mimic*

AMONG BIBLE TEACHERS TODAY there are two principal emphases concerning how a Christian can be sanctified in his daily life. The word *sanctification* need not frighten you. It has a very simple meaning: "to be set apart." The moment you were saved you were sanctified in the sense that you were set apart as belonging to God (1 Cor 6:11). But you are supposed to continue to be set apart to God in all of the practices of daily living. This is the present and progressive aspect of sanctification.

The two emphases concerning the present work of sanctification are these. Some emphasize the "faith" or "rest" side of sanctification. Sometimes this is presented under labels like "the exchanged life" with expressions like "Let Christ live His life through you." Others stress the imitation of Christ or following the Lord. Certainly the Bible teaches the concept of the exchanged life. But it also teaches us that we are to imitate our Lord as a means of sanctification. Listen to these two verses. "For even hereunto were ye called: because Christ also suffered for us, leaving us an example, that ye should follow his steps"

(1 Pet 2:21). "He that saith he abideth in him ought himself also so to walk, even as he walked" (1 John 2:6). These verses clearly indicate the need for imitating the life, activity, interests, motivations, and thoughts of our Lord as we find them in the Word. Although these two verses do not use the specific word *imitate*, other verses do, and the word they use is the equivalent of our English word *mimic*.

If you would look at the few places where the word *mimic* is used, you would find that believers are to imitate good conduct (1 Pet 3:13); good people (Heb 6:12); those who suffer for the Gospel's sake (1 Thess 1:6; 2:14); the apostle Paul (1 Cor 4:16; 11:1); and God (Eph 5:1). In this last verse you discover that the motive for imitating God is that we belong to His family. There is a saying that "imitation is the sincerest form of flattery," and this is true, for a person imitates (not pokes fun at) only those he looks up to. This is illustrated whenever we say, "I want to be like so-and-so."

Obviously one might say many things about this subject of imitation, but I want to speak only of what is involved in a good imitation.

First of all, there must be a pattern. You don't imitate an abstraction; you mimic a concrete reality. Imitation is not based on a good guess; it is based on some objective reality which you look at, carefully observe, and pattern your own imitation after. The imitation of Christ means, of course, that we mimic what we know of the life of Christ. And the only place we can find the facts of His life is in the written record of it in the Bible.

Believe it or not, I used to have a Sunday school teacher who said what was written about the life of Christ in the Bible wasn't important just as long as we imitated Him.

16

When I got a little older I began to ask myself, "How can you imitate Christ unless you know what He did? And how do you know what He did unless you read the Bible?" The only place one can find out anything about the actions and thoughts of the Lord is in the Bible and chiefly in the gospels. If you have never done it you ought to read the gospels sometime and make a list of all the things about Christ which you could imitate in your own life.

Not only can you find a pattern to imitate in the life of Christ, but you may also find one in people. Twice the apostle Paul exhorted his readers to follow his example. (Of course he could say this because he himself followed Christ.) Elsewhere we are told to follow the example of godly Christians (Heb 6:12; 13:7). Actually, since the lives of all of us are seen by others, we all set some sort of pattern for people to follow. Whether we realize it or not, there are others who look to each of us as a pattern to imitate. I often wonder what they see.

The second thing involved in a good imitation is a perusal of the pattern. According to the dictionary, *perusal* means "a careful reading," not a casual reading. The pattern has to be studied in order to have a clear and detailed understanding of all the items included. To imitate the main features of the life of Christ is not enough; our imitation should include the details as well.

At a senior class party, someone stood up and read a list of typical sayings of the various members of the faculty. I'm sure it was not difficult to compile such a list, and I did not have much difficulty recognizing most of the sayings. I certainly had no trouble recognizing the one I apparently use all the time. It is not so difficult to read a list of sayings as it would have been for one of the seniors to imitate a teacher in his actions, speech, mannerisms, gestures, and all the little things that make up a good imitation. A lot of Christians can repeat the sayings of Christ, but they are woefully lacking when it comes to imitating His actions. If you are going to be a good imitator of Christ, you must observe carefully and continuously the details of the life of Christ as recorded in the gospels.

Examples are legion, but one or two will suffice. The way Christians attend church services these days is not a good imitation of the example of Christ. Actually, the conduct of most believers regarding Sunday worship is disgraceful. In addition to the clear command of the Bible to assemble ourselves together (Heb 10:25), the example of Christ with regard to the services of the synagogue of His day should settle the matter once and for all for all Christians. It was His custom to attend the religious services of His day (Luke 4:16). It should also be ours. The question of whether or not you like the preacher is really not relevant. You go to worship God, not the preacher.

Another thing the Lord always did was to offer to help before He was asked. This seems like a small thing, but a good imitation pays attention to small details. Most of us are willing to help if asked; a good mimic of Christ will not wait until he is asked—he will volunteer as soon as he sees the need.

The third thing involved in being a good mimic is practice. Nobody does a good imitation by just looking at the pattern, taking notes, or even writing a script. There has to be constant, faithful, determined practice. In the Christian life this means developing "habits of holiness." Now habits don't develop overnight, but they should be developing all the time. Don't be discouraged if you haven't been able to

18

achieve everything you want to in the Christian life. But you ought to be concerned if there hasn't been any progress in holiness during the past six months.

Personally, I believe the principal problem in trying to develop godly habits is not motivation but determination. Every Christian has within him the motivation of his new nature and his position of being in the family of God. I am inclined to think that today too many people are using their supposed lack of motivation as an excuse for lack of simple determination. I often hear young people exclaim, "This doesn't motivate me, and that's why I can't do it." There are a lot of things that do not motivate me, either, but I have to do them. It is usually not motivation that is lacking; the trouble is that you don't have plain old-fashioned gumption!

When I was taking piano lessons years ago, I had a teacher who used to help me learn difficult passages this way. She would write over the line "three times perfect." That meant that I had to practice the passage until I could play it three times perfectly and consecutively. It did not mean three times during the week between lessons, but consecutively during the course of any practice session. If I played it twice perfectly and made a mistake the third time, I had to start all over. But usually when I succeeded in doing it three times perfectly in practice, I could do it once perfectly in the lesson. Habits of holiness are developed the same way. As you practice, habits are formed, and as habits are formed, they become second nature to you so you can go on to new victories. But it all takes practice, practice, practice.

The last thing involved in a good imitation is the product. A good imitation produces a true replica of the original. So true should it be that it in turn could be imitated by others. That is why Paul was able to exhort his followers to imitate him. He was a replica of his Master. You will not become proud of your good imitation, because a good imitator never draws attention to himself but only to the one he is imitating. If the pattern and the product are the same, people will remember the pattern. If you see a good imitator on television, the chances are you will not remember the name of the imitator, but you will remember whom he imitated. If you are a good mimic of Christ, people will remember the Lord. That's the way it should be.

# 3

## *"What, Me Sin?"*

TAKE A SHORT QUIZ, will you? There are just two questions. I'd like to be able to ask you to raise your hand if the answer to either question is yes, because I'd like to know your immediate reaction.

Here's the first question. Did you sin during the last twenty-four hours? Raise your hand if you did.

Here's the second question. Can you specifically name one sin which you committed in the past twenty-four hours? Raise your hand if you can.

In an audience there would not be so many hands on the second question, because while most of us are willing to admit that we have sinned, not so many are willing to be specific about sinning. It's not so difficult to confess that we are sinners as it is to say, "Lord, I committed such and such a sin." And I'm afraid this insensitivity to specific sins is on the increase. Or if it is not an insensitivity, it's a segregating of certain sins into that category which is all right because it is expected that everyone commits some sins, and other sins into the category which is really sin. We inevitably come to take it for granted that some sins are really not sins, since everybody ought to be allowed to indulge in a few pet sins.

Some time ago I read in the newspaper this observation by a medical doctor speaking at a local mental health conference: "There is no place for the concept of sin in psychotherapy. To introduce this concept is highly precarious. No human being should ever be blamed for anything he does." Shocking, isn't it? But have you ever turned in an assignment that wasn't your work? Or falsified a reading report? Or violated your parents' guidelines?

What is sin? This may seem a bit academic, but I assure you it is necessary. We cannot be sensitive to that about which we are ignorant, though sometimes we make our definition fit our experience or desires, rather than deriving our definition from the Word of God.

Many definitions of sin have been proposed through the centuries, but they all fall into three classes. The first is illustrated by the quotation from the doctor—sin is an illusion; that is, it really does not exist. This is usually attributed to our ignorance, or lack of progress; but for one reason or another, sin is an illusion which we could be rid of by knowledge or evolutionary progress.

The second definition is more theological and conceives of sin as selfishness. Now this is a good definition as far as it goes. Most sin is related to selfishness, but there are some sins which are not selfish at all and which are very definitely sins. For instance, if a father, seeing his family starving, goes out and steals just enough food in order to feed them and not himself, then by this definition he has not sinned because he did not act selfishly. He simply fed his family. But in the process of doing so he became a thief, and that is sin. So you see the definition is all right as far as it goes, but it doesn't go far enough.

Third, there's the biblical definition of sin in 1 John 3:4. Sin is lawlessness. However, this seemingly simple definition needs further explanation, for we won't know what lawlessness is unless we define law. Unless we understand the standard, we will not realize what are the deviations from that standard. What is law? Well, that depends on what period of history you are talking about. Law in the Garden of Eden was one thing; law in the time of Abraham consisted of certain specific ordinances and statutes (Gen 26:5). In the time of Moses, Law meant those 613 specific commandments which God gave the Israelites through him.

Today we also have hundreds of definite commandments under grace, and deviation from any one of those is, according to 1 John 3:4, sin. Some of those commandments are negative; some are positive; some areas of living are governed by principles whose violation is sin. Another area is governed by the leaders of the Church, for in certain matters of conduct God has left it up to the leaders to give guidance (Heb 13:7, 17). But actually all of these commandments and principles stem from the one all-inclusive principle of 1 Corinthians 10:31: "Whether therefore ye eat, or drink, or whatsoever ye do, do all to the glory of God." This is the standard, and not living up to it is sin. You remember that verse you always quote to the sinner: "For all have sinned, and come short of the glory of God" (Rom 3:23). You see, the standard against which sin is measured is the glory of God.

What is the glory of God? It is the showing off of God's character. There is not a thing even in complex twentieth-century life that cannot be tested by this standard. Does it glorify God? Does it show Him off? Therefore, this is an all inclusive definition of sin. Sin is anything contrary to the character of God Himself. That includes anything contrary to His written Word and everything contrary to the character of the living Word, our Lord Jesus Christ.

Having defined sin, may I now remind you of some sins that are peculiar to young people? Here is one. Not doing your own assignments or term papers. It happens even in Christian schools. But turning in someone else's work is just as much stealing as if you took a $10 bill out of someone's pocket. You picked a paper or an assignment out of someone else's brains. Need I say anything about stealing an answer on a test? I know it's done quite regularly by non-Christian young people, and even occasionally by one of God's children. If you are tempted along these lines, I suggest you sit over in the corner by yourself and not expose yourself to such temptation.

Here is another exam week sin, and it is one that the Lord Himself condemned—useless speaking. Now this usually happens when we are under extra pressure. Most of us when we are rested are not bothered by this sin. It is just when we become tired and the pressure becomes extra heavy.

Here is a third one—fruitlessness. Don't let studying be an excuse for not witnessing. And may I remind you that the reverse is also true. Do not let witnessing be an excuse for not studying. Just discipline yourself, cut out the horseplay, and you will have time for both. And through it all remember that the fruit of the spirit is patience—that is, endurance—perseverance, and self-control. It is very easy to indulge in impatience during exam week, for instance, and rave about leaving school because it is not worth it and you can serve the Lord somewhere else. No endurance. All out of breath after just one semester.

Finally, I want to remind you of two effects of sin—any sin. The first is this: Every sin becomes a part of your personal history. You can confess it, God will forgive you, it will be remembered in condemnation against you no more, but it is still part of your personal history. If you fail a course, you can and should confess it, but it is still on your record. If you do not study to your capacity, you may pass the course, but it will always be a fact of history that you did not learn certain things that you should have. May I illustrate with something not related to school?

I was reared near St. Louis in the old days when there were two major league ball clubs there—the Cards and the Browns. One day my dad said to my brother and me, "Do you want to go to the ball game tomorrow?" Of course we wanted to go. But before tomorrow came I got mad at my father. So I said, "I'll show him. I won't go to the ball game with him." And I didn't. Now, my father and I made up. He forgave me. But I never saw that ball game, and I never will. What you do today will be history tomorrow, and sin affects your personal record.

The second effect is this: Sin grieves God. It grieves your heavenly Father when you sin. Let this be a deterrent when you are tempted to sin. I once had a club of boys twelve to fourteen years old. These fellows were Christians and had grown quite a bit in the Christian life. One day I was trying to explain to them, on the basis of 1 John 1 and 2, what happened when a Christian sinned. I told them how Satan accused them, how absolutely right he was, and how the Lord Jesus stood up as their Advocate or

Lawyer and took their case defending it on the single basis that He paid for that sin by His death on the cross of Calvary. When I finished, one of the fellows said to me, "You know, if what you have said is true, it certainly must grieve God because I have to confess to Him so often. I think I'll just try not to sin so much."

And I thought he got the point. Do you?

# 4

## *The Sin of Independence*

TODAY I WANT to tell you a fable. It's about a watch. You see, once upon a time there was a certain watch. It was a very beautiful watch, and it was extremely useful to its owner because it kept time accurately. Inside this watch were a lot of parts, including many big wheels and little wheels.

One fine day when everything was going so well and the watch was doing its job so efficiently, one of those little wheels inside that watch got an idea. He said to himself, "I'm as good and as necessary as any other part. I ought to be a big wheel. As a matter of fact, I'm getting tired of always being a little wheel constantly being kicked in the teeth. If I can't be a big wheel, I'll be independent. I'll show them. I'll come out from among them and be separate!"

And he did just that.

He detached himself from all the other wheels and parts and became independent. And do you know what happened? Very quickly and very surely he ground to a screeching halt, and he found himself good for nothing. Nevertheless, the little wheel had achieved his purpose— he had shown them. He had gained independence, but at the terrible price of uselessness. Not only had he made himself of no value, but he had upset every other part, and he had rendered the watch useless to its owner.

That's the fable. Do you get the point? Independence can be a sin. But just in case someone is thinking, *Well, thank the Lord, at last he has seen the light and is going to talk about the evils of separationism,* I would ask you not to get too comfortable. Actually, I am not speaking about ecclesiastical separationism at all, but about personal independence.

This fable has scriptural basis. Our Lord said just before His crucifixion, "Abide in me, and I in you. As the branch cannot bear fruit of itself, except it abide in the vine; no more can ye, except ye abide in me. I am the vine, ye are the branches: he that abideth in me, and I in him, the same bringeth forth much fruit: for *without me ye can do nothing*" (John 15:4-5, italics added).

The fact of the matter is, our Lord said we cannot be independent of Him except at the expense of life itself. And without life, of what use are we? So life and usefulness depend on dependence on Christ. Furthermore, He said on another occasion, "Take my yoke upon you, and learn of me" (Matt 11:29). Most people do not like to be yoked to anything, but Christ said this is the way to learn of Him.

The sin of independence, or the sin of not abiding in Christ, or the sin of disengaging ourselves from the yoke of Christ takes many forms in our personal lives. I want to remind you of three.

The first goes like this: "I don't need anybody's help. I can stand on my own two feet." Now, of course, there are a million things wrong with such a statement, one of which is simply this. If we do not need to help each other, then why did God give the gift of helps to the Body of Christ? (Read 1 Corinthians 12:28). If you can be so self-sufficient as not to need the help of any other Christian, then you might as well tell the Lord that He made a mistake in giving the spiritual gift of helps. Further, why did the Lord say, "Restore such an one in the spirit of meekness" (Gal 6:1), if we do not need to help one another? He says we need integration, not independence.

The second form this sin takes with some young people is this: "I don't need a school laying down rules for me." And then soon this independent person graduates to this: "I don't need a mission board telling me what to do." In other words, independence becomes anarchy. The fact of the matter is that the Lord Himself, the Head of the Church, has given rulers to His Church to govern its members (Heb 13:7, 17). If there are God-given rulers, then there are God-expected followers. And the ruled are expected to obey the rulers. Let's face it, young people, wisdom comes, in the normal course of events, with age and experience, and you need the wisdom of older deans of men and women, and mission board members, to help you in your service for the Lord. Remember, anarchy is a kissing cousin to independence, and it's a kiss of death.

Here's a third form the sin takes: "I don't need any advice. After all, I can get my orders from the Lord directly, just like these Christians who are always giving me advice." If this is true, then why do we read in the second chapter of Titus that the older women are to teach the young women "to be sober, to love their husbands, to love their children, to be discreet, chaste, keepers at home, good, obedient to their own husbands," and that the older men are to instruct the young men "to be sober minded"

29

(vv. 4-6)? Beware of any course of action which is contrary to the advice of older Christians. Now I grant you that there are times when you may have to go against all advice, but be careful that doing so is not just a cover-up for unyieldedness, disobedience, or independence. It is all too easy to "see" the Lord's will in ours—to say something is His will because it is ours. It ought to be the other way around. Our thinking should reflect God's will and God's mind. Too often we make up our own minds, ignore the sound advice of our superiors, tell the Lord this must be His will, and, like the little wheel, come to a screeching halt—absolutely no good to anybody.

Finally, I want to say something about the folly of this sin of independence. First Corinthians 12 explains clearly why we need integration in the Body of Christ. Paul lists some of the various spiritual gifts (vv. 4-11). Then he reminds us that every gift is necessary and illustrates that fact with the human body (vv. 12-25). Then he very vividly shows how we must work together in the Body of Christ (vv. 26-31). In the latter part of this chapter we see, by contrast, some of the consequences of the sin of independence. Will you notice three?

First, we will show no sympathy to other believers (v. 26). We are supposed to suffer with those who suffer, and rejoice with those who are honored. But usually independence twists us so that we rejoice over those who suffer and suffer over those who are honored. Criticism replaces sympathy.

Second, we will have no concern for other Christians (v.25b). We are to be integrated so that "the members should have the same care one for another." But if you have cut yourself off from other Christians, then all you care about is yourself and your own little sphere of activities and the little clique you may have attracted to yourself. Sometimes that circle which is drawn includes only yourself, sometimes only a boy or girl friend, sometimes just a small group of other Christians. In any case, we become careless about others when we are concerned only with ourselves.

Third, there will be division in the Body of Christ. Working together guards against schism in the body (v. 25a). This can happen in a school, in a mission, or in a church, and wherever it happens weakness inevitably follows. Like the watch, the group is weakened when anyone refuses to do his part. In unity is strength.

I'm sure that most of you have seen pictures of the San Francisco-Oakland Bay bridge in California. Once when I was riding across it with someone, the driver informed me that the cables which support the bridge are made of piano wire. When he told me that, I was tempted to jump out of the car, for I have been at piano recitals when the artist by simply hitting a soft felt hammer against a piano wire has broken it. And there I was trusting my life and lives of all those other people in the hundreds of cars on that bridge to piano wire! But I calmed down when I was reminded that the cable was not a single wire but a lot of them woven together. In this way there was both flexibility and strength in the cable sufficient to support two eight-lane decks of rush-hour traffic.

It's the same with Christians. You can put yourself in the company of other believers and work with them, strengthening yourself and the work of God in this earth, or you can separate yourself and become useless and hurtful to others. This can happen in your school, in your young people's group, or in your church. All you have to do is say, "I don't need any help; I don't need any ruling; I don't need any advice." But be warned. If you say that, you're vulnerable. If you want strength and usefulness, then learn the virtues of dependence—dependence first on the risen Lord and then on one another.

# 5

## *What About Getting Married?*

WHAT DO YOU THINK of a Christian who puts the making of money before the Lord's work? You don't think he's much of a Christian, do you?

What would you think of someone who was so happy that he couldn't settle down and really serve the Lord? Well, you don't often see such a person, though once in a while you meet the kind of person who seemingly can never be sober. Again you would say that such a person was off the track spiritually.

Here's a third question. What would you think of someone who gets so sorrowful, depressed, dejected, and discouraged because of some circumstances in his life that he cannot do anything for the Lord? Again you would say that individual was wrong, that he ought to be able to live above the circumstances so they would not interfere with his serving the Lord.

In all of these cases you easily recognize that something—either things, joy, or sorrow—has come between the believer and his Lord. You readily see that possessions, gladness, or sorrow must not take precedence over the Lord's work.

But what do you say to this question: Should marriage hinder your doing the Lord's work?

That one is not so easy to answer, is it? I suppose most of you want to fudge and answer, "That depends." And that means it depends on whether or not you are thinking about getting married.

I find it takes some courage to deal with 1 Corinthians 7, but it is just as much a part of the teaching of the Word of God for the believer today as 1 Corinthians 13 or any other appropriate passage, so we must not ignore it.

There are three questions asked and answered in this chapter—though I am not referring to the questions I just asked you, but to three basic questions which form the outline of the entire passage.

The chapter was written, of course, to answer some questions which the Corinthians had evidently written to Paul. We do not have their side of the correspondence, and therefore we are, so to speak, listening to only one side of a two-way conversation. Nevertheless, we must not use this as an excuse for avoiding the clear teaching of the chapter. Haven't you ever been in a room where somebody was talking on the telephone and haven't you been pretty much able to follow the entire conversation even though you could only hear one person speaking? It wasn't hard to piece together what was being said on the other end—especially if you were intensely interested in the subject being discussed. Don't let the fact that 1 Corinthians 7 is only one side of the correspondence deceive you into thinking you can't understand its meaning. Actually, it isn't what I do *not* understand about this

34

chapter's background that bothers me; rather, it is what is so clearly taught in the passage that concerns me.

I said there were three questions. The first is this: Is marriage preferred (vv. 1-9)?

The answer is yes and no. It does depend in this instance upon the case. May I simply call your attention to verse 7: "But every man hath his proper gift of God, one after this manner, and another after that." "This manner" was Paul's own marital condition—that is, single—and "that manner" was the opposite condition—married. The gift of God might be either to remain single or to be married. Thus, marriage is not necessarily preferred, for the gift of God in your case might very well be the unmarried state. This is quite clear from verse 8, where Paul declares that it is good for the unmarried to abide in that condition, even as he did.

But for others marriage is preferred. This is so because of certain natural desires discussed in verses 2-6. However, with the fulfillment of these desires comes responsibility, and the responsibility must be discharged with equal unselfishness on the part of both husband and wife. Now I think, fellows, that this ought to be emphasized particularly to us. So often I hear young men say half jokingly concerning marrying some girl, "Well, think of all the help she will be to me! Why, she can type my term papers, and . . . ." But I seldom hear a young man say, "Think of what I can do for her!" And yet these privileges and responsibilities of marriage are to be enjoyed and discharged on a reciprocal basis.

Is marriage preferred? That depends.

The second question of the chapter is this: Is marriage permanent? This is discussed in verses 10 to 24 and 39 to

35

40. The answer to this is an unequivocal yes. Oh, but you say Paul does speak of "departing" in these verses. Yes, but examine the cases. In the case of Christian people, that is, when both husband and wife are believers, he says there should be no divorce (v. 10). Indeed, he says this is the teaching of the Lord Jesus, too. "Let not the wife depart from her husband . . . and let not the husband put away his wife." The standard as far as Christian couples are concerned is *no divorce at all.* Now, he does admit that there may be some circumstance under which there would be a separation, but if that does occur there should be no divorce following.

However, there might be a case of a married couple— both unsaved—who heard the Gospel and only one partner received Christ. In other words, a spiritually mixed marriage, where the mixture occurred after the marriage.

This is not the case of a person who deliberately goes out and marries an unsaved person. God distinctly forbids this (2 Cor 6:14), and anyone who disobeys God's command will have to suffer the consequences. And yet it is surprising in this confused day to find many Christian young people knowingly dating and subsequently marrying unsaved persons. It usually starts with the false reasoning that "it's only a date. I'll break off before it goes too far." Or "I know he is unsaved, but I'll win him to Christ before I get too serious." Beware! If you are going to play with fire, you are sure to get burned. Don't run to God after it is too late. Obey His Word now! But in case the mixture occurs after the marriage, Paul gives some principles for proper conduct in this instance (1 Cor 7:12-16).

But suppose one partner dies? Paul says that it is perfectly all right to be married when the original marriage is

36

broken by death (vv. 39-40). But he hastens to add that he thinks it would be better if the second marriage did not take place.

Both of these exceptional instances—spiritually mixed marriages and remarriages after death—should not make us forget the answer to the principal question of this section. Is marriage permanent? Yes.

Now the third question in the chapter is this: Is marriage paramount (vv. 25-38)? Is marriage the main thing that a Christian ought to consider? And the clear answer to this is: No, it is not.

Now we come back to the questions with which I sneaked up on you at the beginning of this chapter. Should sorrow interfere with serving the Lord? "They that weep, as though they wept not" (v. 30). Should joy? "They that rejoice, as though they rejoiced not" (v. 30). Should money or possessions or business? "They that buy, as though they possessed not" (v. 30). And now we have the climax. Should marriage interfere with doing the Lord's work? Definitely not. It is just as wrong for marriage to interfere as business, sorrow, or joy. This is true whether you are married or not. Listen: "It remaineth, that . . . they that have wives be as though they had none" (v. 29). That's a strange word, isn't it? But the meaning is clear. The Lord should be first—not the husband or wife.

Why so? For two reasons. First, the time is short (v. 29). And if the time to do the Lord's work was short in Paul's day, it is even shorter today. Second, the work is demanding of our first interests (vv. 31-32). Pleasing the Lord should be our first concern, not pleasing our husbands or wives or, I may add, our girl or boy friends. Worldliness is not just the love of things; it may also be the love of persons when that takes precedence over love and service for the Lord.

Now, finally, three general observations about the teaching of this chapter.

First, there is a large place in the Lord's work for the single worker. Anyone who says that there is no such place for a single worker here at home or on the mission field needs to study this chapter. There are some things that a person can do single that he cannot do married. If God leads you this way, don't hang your head in shame.

Second, no Christian should ever entertain for even a moment the notion that if his marriage doesn't work out he can simply go ahead and get a divorce.

Third, it may very well be that God's will for you is to postpone marriage for a while for the sake of the Lord's work. The important thing as far as marriage and the Lord's work are concerned is the Lord's work, not marriage. I shudder when I hear a young person say, "Well, we can't wait; we'll just take the consequences." Can't you wait for your Lord's sake? And incidentally, she might be a better girl if she waits and works for a while. She'll know how to manage things and handle money better; and you might be a better man if you get your education first. Could it be God's will for you to postpone your plans for marriage for His sake? When you point a finger at someone who is so interested in business that the Lord's work suffers, be sure that you shouldn't be pointing a finger at yourself for being so concerned about getting a mate that your work for the Lord suffers also.

# 6

## *Symphonic Dating*

HAVING JUST TALKED about marriage in the preceding chapter it would seem appropriate now to say some things about dating. Indeed, one might say the subjects go hand in hand! Dating has become so prominent a part of our culture that it has almost become a way of life. This probably makes it more imperative that a Christian young person think seriously about many aspects of dating in order to integrate it into his Christian way of life. I thought it would be helpful to think about the subject in terms of a symphony.

If you have ever been to a symphony concert, you know that before there can be any harmonious music there has to be a good bit of tuning up. As a matter of fact, it sometimes sounds like bedlam for five or ten minutes before the program begins. But all of this is a necessary prelude to the finished production. Dating is something like that time of tuning up. It's a time of testing and discovering with a view to finding the one with whom you may spend the rest of your life. In a certain sense, then, every date is a potential marriage.

I have two suggestions about this "tuning up" type of dating. The first is this: Incorporate a lot of variety in your dating. This means not only in the ones you date but also in what you do. There are a lot of interesting people in your school or church circle, and you want to become acquainted with a number of them under a variety of circumstances. You may find that underneath a shy exterior is a sparkling personality, and various situations and activities will reveal many sides of both your personalities. And of course one of the benefits of dating is being able to see all the facets of the character of the one you are dating.

The second suggestion is this: double-date frequently. This is healthy for everyone concerned, and it promotes the kind of exposure you want to have in dating. Now I know you always want to be alone, and sometimes that is perfectly in order. But remember, not too much of that and especially not too soon.

A second thing I want you to consider in this whole matter is part of what I said in the last chapter. Some people ought to go through life solo. Not everybody should expect to enjoy a duet. The New Testament accords a place of honor to the single person—something not true in the Old Testament or in other cultures of the day. There is a place for the single person in the Lord's work, and it is an honored place. Indeed, there are some things a single person can do for God that a married person cannot simply because the married person has certain responsibilities and obligations which demand his time and attention. Furthermore, it might be that the Lord wants you to play it solo for a while before you consider the duet. There may be education to complete or a foreign language to learn on the mission field or some debts to pay off before you consider assuming the obligations of marriage. You won't die if you wait, and you both may be more mature individuals if you do. Thinking about these things need not keep you from dating, but you ought to think about them as you date.

A third aspect of this symphony I want you to consider is this: Who is the conductor? No orchestra in the world ever has two people conducting at the same time, and no marriage can ever be successful with that arrangement. Frankly, I do not feel that the problems we see today along these lines in Christian homes (or even Christian churches) are due to women being out of place, but rather, to men not being in their place. So let me speak directly to you fellows. You are to be the conductor. This does not mean dictator, but it does mean leader. Now, the leader makes some very basic decisions. He determines what to do, how fast to go, the purpose, and the quality of the performance. These are your responsibilities in relation to casual girl friends, steady girl friends, and eventually to your wives. You are the leader, you set the pace, you determine the goals and effect the procedures to bring them to pass. And if things go wrong, ultimately some or all of the blame falls on you.

This leadership responsibility rests upon you fellows in dates. It rests upon you in physical matters, and this means you are responsible not only for the conduct of your bodies but also your dates'. I think the best advice in this realm for all your personal relationships is found in these words of the apostle Paul: "Neither yield ye your members as instruments of unrighteousness unto sin: but yield . . . your members as instruments of righteousness unto God" (Rom 6:13). Symphonic dating results from righteous ac-

41

tions. You will never regret having lived a clean life, but you will regret the opposite. A lifetime of regret is a lot to mortgage for a few moments of illicit abandon.

You men are the leaders, too, in spiritual matters. Unfortunately, this is usually not the case. Think for a moment of some of the Christian families you know. In how many of them do you find the wife asking the husband to explain the meaning of Bible verses? In how many of them does the father lead the family in prayer and worship? Or is it usually the mother who knows the answers and takes the lead? Now, of course, women ought to know their Bibles and pray with their families, but they should not have to direct the spiritual well-being of the family because the husband has abdicated his place of leadership. This usually does not happen overnight. It often begins when young people are in school, when fellows lose interest in the Bible, or when fellows or girls sacrifice spiritual standards because they are afraid they will not get enough dates. There are things worse than not having a date this weekend, and one of them is having a date with someone whose standards are low.

There is one other very important feature about a good symphony, and that is harmony. If God gives you a life partner with whom you have perfect harmony, you can count it one of your greatest blessings. Of course there can be no harmony in a spiritually mixed marriage. Make no mistake about it—God does not approve of marriage between a believer and an unbeliever (1 Cor 6:14). But harmony is made up of little things, too. Suppose I put this tiny stone in my shoe. I hardly feel it. As a matter of fact, I can walk for quite a while and scarcely notice it. But how do you suppose my foot will feel tonight if I leave it in all day?

42

Do you get the point? A little matter can be very annoying after a long time.

But I know many of you do not want to make any mistakes in these matters of dating and marriage. Be assured that God will honor your pure motives and sincere desires. Martin Luther said that parents ought to pray about the life partners of their children as soon as they are born. I think that is good advice, and we may carry it a step further and suggest that you ought to be praying about the matter regularly yourselves. Just be sure your prayer is for His will, not yours.

# 7

## *Satan's Counterfeit*

WHENEVER ONE SPEAKS of Satan these days, it seems
advisable to preface the remarks with some word about
the reality of the existence of Satan. Some Christians
apparently feel that Satan merely exists in the minds of
men and that our thought about his existence is the only
real existence he has. In other words, they say Satan has no
actual, objective existence in his own right. The Scriptures
teach us, however, that Satan existed long before man was
even created (Ezek 28:13-15). Further, every reference by
Christ to the evil one is a proof of his real existence (cf. Matt
13:39; 25:41; Luke 10:18; John 12:31; 16:11). Modern
theology explains such references as accommodation of
the Lord's language to the customary Jewish belief. But it
should be realized that such accommodation in this area
would invalidate His entire message.

In addition, Christians sometimes forget that Satan can
transform himself in a variety of ways. On the one hand, he
presents himself as an angel of light and his ministers as
ministers of righteousness, not unrighteousness (2 Cor

11:14-15). On the other hand, the Scriptures picture him, at least in one place, as a dragon with horns and a tai¹ (Rev 12:3-4). This is a representation of his fierce nature and of the death struggle in which he is engaged with God's people.

But whatever particular representation Satan makes of himself, he has a single purpose in his program. His purpose, aim, and goal is simply to counterfeit the will of God. This has been, presently is, and always will be his purpose as long as he has freedom.

Counterfeiting also has a single purpose. It is simply to create something as similar to the original as possible and to do it by means of some shortcut. A counterfeit is similar but cheap. A counterfeit United States dollar bill, for instance, does not have a picture of Abraham Lincoln on it. This would be a sure sign that it was counterfeit. It will have Washington's picture and it will be as near to a genuine bill in as many details as possible, except that there will be some deceptive shortcut—either a poor engraving or cheaper paper or ink. But the point is that when you make a counterfeit you make it like the original, not unlike it.

This is the most important fact to understand about Satan's purpose in this world. If he is the master counterfeiter, then he is trying to do something that is similar to the will of God, not dissimilar. This is particularly important for Christians to grasp. Satan is intelligent enough to know that if he puts something in the Christian's path, perhaps some temptation, which is obviously not the will of God, the Christian will be alert to it and resist it. But if he can offer something good which, though good in itself, is not the best, then he will be more likely to gain the advantage.

In Satan's first act of sin he boldly announced this

45

counterfeit policy. It was expressed in five statements beginning with "I will," the last of which summarized his policy in these words: "I will be like the most High" (Isa 14:14). The important thing to notice is, of course, that Satan did not propose to be unlike God, but to be like Him. He intended to oppose God by counterfeit. From the very beginning this was his openly declared purpose.

Satan's first attempt to pass a counterfeit plan to man was made in the Garden of Eden. His lure was this: "Yea, hath God said, Ye shall not eat of every tree of the garden?" (Gen 3:1). The emphasis was on the word *every*. We know this from the reply which first came to Eve's mind, namely, "We may eat of the fruit of the trees of the garden" (Gen 3:2). Satan's bait was to try to get Eve to think of the fact that God should give them everything. There should be no restrictions in the perfect plan of a good God. Eve's reply showed that she felt that for all practical purposes God had given them everything: "We may eat of the fruit of the trees of the garden," in other words, "Of course, God has given us everything." Only then did it occur to her that there was one restriction, so she added, almost as an afterthought, "But of the fruit of the tree which is in the midst of the garden, God hath said, Ye shall not eat of it, neither shall ye touch it, lest ye die" (Gen 3:3). The important point is not whether this was an addition to God's Word. I doubt that it was. God had very likely said this to Adam and Eve during one of their evening walks in the garden. Also, it is difficult to view "neither shall ye touch it" as an addition to God's Word, because Eve must have been reporting the truth since before the Fall she could not have told a lie. The important point to notice in this conversation is simply that Satan succeeded in centering Eve's thoughts on **the single restriction**. This was the beginning of the end.

Actually, the restriction which forbade Adam and Eve to eat of the fruit of the one tree of the knowledge of good and evil was both a major and a minor one. It was a major thing simply because it was *the* test of their obedience or disobedience to the will of God. In contrast to our situation today in which we can sin hundreds of different ways, Adam and Eve could only sin in one way—by eating of this fruit. It was a major thing then because it involved the entire matter of their obedience to the will of God. But in another way it must have been a very minor thing. In the everyday course of their lives, this single restriction played no important part. Out of all the trees in the Garden of Eden, of all the variety and expansiveness of God's provision for them, to restrict one tree was relatively a very minor thing. It is not difficult to imagine that in the course of some days Adam and Eve may not have passed by the tree of the knowledge of good and evil. Perhaps even in the course of weeks it did not come into their experience. In this respect it was a relatively inconsequential thing, since it was only one tree out of many. This is probably why it did not occur to Eve to mention the restriction when she first replied to the serpent. It came to her almost as an after-thought, as recorded in verse 3.

What sort of a counterfeit was this? It was an attempt to counterfeit the goodness of God. "If God were good," Satan was saying, "He would not withhold anything from you. But since He has held back the fruit of a single tree, He cannot be good. In contrast," Satan tantalized, "my plan allows you to do the very thing God will not permit."

Perhaps this counterfeiting approach can best be illustrated by pointing out the logic involved. This was the approach of a syllogism, that is, a major premise, a minor premise, and a conclusion. The well-known collegiate example of a syllogism is this: major premise—all students are poor; minor premise—I am a student; conclusion—I am poor. The syllogism underlying Satan's approach to Eve was simply this: major premise—all restrictions are evil; minor premise—God's plan is restrictive; conclusion—God's plan is evil. "Hath God said, Ye shall not eat of *every* tree of the garden?" If God restricted even one tree, then God's plan is evil because restrictions are evil.

Of course, the conclusion of any syllogism is only as accurate as its premise. Let us examine, therefore, Satan's premise. Restrictions are evil, he said. At one time or another, and concerning some circumstance or another, most of us have subscribed to this premise, restrictions are evil. In the minds of students there is not the shadow of a doubt as to the validity of this premise. Imagine asking grown, adult, mature young people to be inside a building at a certain time of night! Or why should there be deadlines on assignments and term papers? After all, what difference does it make if mine is just one day late? The teacher cannot possibly grade all of them at once. And then there is that monstrous thing called academic probation, which restricts the extra-curricular participation of those who may be on such probation. Students will readily assent to the proposition that restrictions are evil. But are they? When young people grow into the responsibility of parenthood, they are quite glad to be assured that their own children will not be roaming the streets of a city any time of night. And even students realize in their sober moments that the

restrictions concerning assignments and papers are necessary, otherwise they would never get them done. The
restrictions of a schedule are necessary and good for all of
us. Failing a course is worse than the restrictions of its
requirements to pass. Being caught unprepared is worse
than the restrictions of a schedule.

Are restrictions evil? No one would care to have all the
traffic laws in our country suddenly rescinded. And surely
we would not sleep comfortably tonight if we knew that all
the restricting bars of the zoos of this country had been
removed. Restrictions are evil, Satan said. God's plan is
restrictive; thus God's plan is evil.

Satan is still promoting this same counterfeit today. Here
are two illustrations in the spiritual realm. Our Lord Jesus
said, "I am the way, the truth, and the life: no man cometh
unto the Father, but by me" (John 14:6). This is obviously
a very restricted plan of salvation. Satan's plan allows men
to "come to God" in any way they please. In order to pass
off this counterfeit, he appeals to man's pride by suggesting to him that he is capable of deciding for himself and
doesn't need to be told what is right or what is wrong.
Restrictions are evil. God's plan of salvation is restrictive (as
it is). Therefore, God's plan is to be rejected and Satan's
accepted.

Satan comes to the young Christian with the same
counterfeit that he used in Eden. He says, "Has God given
you everything as a Christian?" The immediate response
is, "Certainly, yes." And then some of the things that have
been gladly given up for Christ's sake come to mind, and
the mind begins to dwell on them. Soon all that is seen are
the few restrictions which originally were gladly given up
and quickly forgotten in view of all the riches of grace in

Christ. It is an easy step from "I *don't* do this" to "I *can't* do this," and an easier one to "*Why* can't I do this?"

So it was with Eve. She took Satan's bait and began to major on the minor restriction. She was then softened up for the next phase of his attack. It is recorded in Genesis 3:4-5: "And the serpent said unto the woman, Ye shall not surely die: for God doth know that in the day ye eat thereof, then your eyes shall be opened, and ye shall be as gods, knowing good and evil." It goes without saying—or does it?—that Satan did not promise Eve that if she followed him her life would be shortened and she would become like the devil himself. He promised her long existence and that she would be like God.

To review: Satan's first step was to plant the idea in Eve's mind that restrictions are evil; and since God's plan for her and Adam was restrictive, God's plan was evil. His second step was to offer her the counterfeit plan, that is, his own substitute, which promised no restrictions, but rather, that she could be like God and not die. The third step Eve took on her own. It was the step of rationalizing the wrong she was about to do. "And when the woman saw that the tree was good for food, and that it was pleasant to the eyes, and a tree to be desired to make one wise, she took of the fruit thereof, and did eat, and gave also unto her husband with her; and he did eat" (Gen 3:6). She began to examine the forbidden fruit and to notice all the "good" things about it. After all, she reasoned, wasn't it good for food, and didn't God want them to eat? And shouldn't a woman want to set good food before her husband for his nourishment? Then she reflected on its beauty, and of course the same line of argument applied in this respect, too. God created a lot of beauty in this world. Why should He withhold this beauti-

50

ful fruit? Finally she reasoned that since wisdom is desirable (and it is), and since the fruit would make her wise, it must be desirable to eat the fruit. Gone from her mind was the central fact that God had expressly forbidden the eating of this particular fruit. Quickly forgotten was His specific command. Gone from her thought was the promise of death for disobedience. Her mind was filled only with the rationalizations—the fruit would give physical sustenance, it would cultivate their aesthetic tastes, and it would add to their wisdom. Having prejustified her action, Eve ate in flagrant disobedience to the revealed will of God.

Here were two important ramifications of her action. The first is stated in verse 6: she "gave also unto her husband with her; and he did eat." It is simply this: Her sin affected someone else. And, of course, Adam's sin has affected the entire race. All sin affects others in some way or another. We do not live in a vacuum, and what we do or neglect to do affects others. Failure to maintain regular prayer time, for instance, will definitely affect those lives for whom you do not pray. Failure to persevere in the study of the Word will affect the quality of your life and testimony. All that we do or fail to do affects others in some way.

The second observation concerning this act is this: Once the sin was done it could never be undone. History cannot be erased. Forgiveness can be secured, and fellowship can be restored, but history cannot be changed. This is one of the most important lessons we can ever learn about sin. I suppose every teacher has seen the reality of this many times. A student writes back years later to apologize for not paying attention in the teacher's class, and he sincerely asks forgiveness. Of course, the teacher forgives, and that forgiveness is fully and sincerely given, but that forgiveness

51

does not restore the opportunity of those classes or put notes in a blank notebook or place good grades on a poor transcript. What we do today will forever be a part of today's history. Adam's sin has changed history, but history cannot change the fact of Adam's sin. Every human being in the world today is living proof that sin affects others and that history cannot be erased.

This makes us realize more than ever the importance of being in the will of God and not accepting Satan's counterfeit. Knowing the will of God is conditioned on three things (Rom 12:1-2). First, there must be the complete and conclusive presentation of one's life. This is not salvation but dedication, and it concerns the matter of whom you will serve with the years of your life. Second, there must be separation from the world. And third, there must be that transformation which the Holy Spirit wants to effect in every believer's life. Then—and only then—can one know that good, acceptable, and perfect will of God.

Satan's counterfeit will, or God's genuine will—this is the choice. Sometimes it becomes easier to determine God's will if consideration is given to the alternative, namely, Satan's will, which will always come in the form of a counterfeit—something like the genuine article but involving some shortcut. May God give His people in these days keen discernment to see His will and zealous desire to do it.

# 8

## *Smart or Simple?*

CONCERNING EVIL THESE DAYS, it is apparently smart to be smart. And it is considered simple to be simple about things which are sinful. To be practiced in sin is smart; to be ignorant of it or inexperienced in it is simple.

Although this attitude is frequently exhibited by Christians, God says it is absolutely wrong. Concerning evil, it is only smart to be simple. "I would have you wise unto that which is good, and simple concerning evil" (Rom 16:19).

The word *simple* appears only in two other places in the New Testament. In both places (Matt 10:16; Phil 2:15) it is wrongly translated "harmless." The mistranslation assumes a wrong derivation of the word, while the translation "simple" in Romans 16:19 is correct. Literally, it means "unmixed, or free from foreign matter" like an unalloyed metal. In Greek papyri it is translated by the words *pure* and *purity*. In other words, to be simple concerning evil is to be free, unmixed, and pure in relation to it.

This is not easy to do today when evil is paraded everywhere—even sometimes in Christian circles. There is the new convert's testimony. The greater the sin from which he has been saved, the greater the show. It is not always the convert's fault that this happens; too often the blame rests squarely on Christian leaders who exploit him. This is not always true, of course, for many testimonies genuinely glorify God and not the convert or the sin from which he was saved. But sometimes harmful exploitation of the babe in Christ continues for months and years. The result to the convert is that he does not grow in the Lord, for months later he is still giving the same testimony he gave the week after he was saved. The result to those who hear him is that they become educated concerning evil.

There is the printed page. One month's issue of a well-known Christian magazine contained thirteen articles. Of the thirteen, eight paraded the evils of the past in titles such as these: "I Became an Addict," "From 'Carmen' to Christ," "I Resented My Brother," "I Was a Musical Comedian." What about the person who did not practice all kinds of evil? What about the child converted early in life through the efforts of his godly parents? Did it not take just as much of the grace of God to save these as those who experienced the depths of sin? And do not their conversions glorify the Lord just as much as the others?

And then there are older Christians who become young people's leaders, or alumni who come back to their alma mater. The young people and the students easily get the impression that if they want to be spiritual giants like these leaders and alumni, they too must indulge in the pranks and breaking of rules which their leaders did in their day. And the young people have no difficulty learning what the best pranks are in minute detail. Their examples in faith become their teachers in folly. To explain that it is only natural is to admit that it is Adamic, sinful, and contrary to the Word of God. The Scripture says young people are to be taught to be sober, not foolish (Titus 2:4, 6). May God give us young people's leaders and alumni of Christian schools who, if they themselves have been foolish in their youth, will have sense enough to remember that silence is golden.

But, someone may say, you are basing a lot on one phrase in the Bible. Do not forget that other Scriptures present the same truth. "And have no fellowship with the unfruitful works of darkness, but rather reprove them. For it is a shame even to speak of those things which are done of them in secret" (Eph 5:11-12). "Finally, brethren, whatsoever things are true, whatsoever things are honest, whatsoever things are just, whatsoever things are pure, whatsoever things are lovely, whatsoever things are of good report; if there be any virtue, and if there be any praise, think on these things" (Phil 4:8). Here is the secret of being "wise unto that which is good, and simple concerning evil." Since it is true that as a man "thinketh in his heart, so is he" (Prov 23:7), the believer's thought life becomes the key. The child of God should occupy his mind with things truthful (not merely true factually but truthful ethically), honest, or honorable in the sense that they might be revered, just, and right in the sight of God and man, pure or chaste, lovely or pleasing and winsome, and of good report or attractive. These not only are criteria for our thinking but may properly be applied to new converts' testimonies, articles for publication, and the speech of youth leaders and alumni. In Philippians 4:9, Paul dares to point to his own life as an example of this kind of thinking with its resultant action.

Certainly there are occasions when we must expose the works of darkness, but such reproof does not include glamorizing or parading them. We should be careful about washing our dirty clothes in public or violating decency in the name of reality or truthfulness. Telling the truth is not always telling everything one knows. There are still occasions in this twentieth century when "charity [love] shall cover the multitude of sins" (1 Peter 4:8). In this day when evil in all its many forms is on parade all around us, we need to concentrate on being simple toward it and on cultivating and promoting such simplicity in others. Concerning evil, it's smart to be simple.

# 9

## *Foolish Questions*

IN MY YEARS OF TEACHING I have discovered that sometimes it is good for students to ask questions and sometimes it is good not to have questions. When I taught freshmen in seminary, I used to tell them on the very first day that I appreciated questions as long as they were honest questions. But freshmen in graduate school know more even than freshmen in college, and their questions are not always honest. Some were, but others were asked, I am sure, in order to show me how much the questioner knew or to show off to his fellow students his vast knowledge. Sometimes, of course, the questions were asked in order to pit me against another professor. Sometimes it is good to have questions and sometimes it is not.

Today I want to talk to you about some foolish questions. They fall into two categories: questions that are *ignorant* and questions that are *impertinent*.

First, I want to give you a couple of illustrations from the Scriptures. The record in Mark 12 shows the Lord Jesus being put on the spot a number of times during a certain day. One of the groups that came to him was the Sadducees. They had concocted a most fanciful, theoretical, impossible illustration about a man who died childless and whose brother married the widow and also died childless and whose brother married the widow and also died, until seven brothers had finally married the same wife. Now, you see this illustration was based on truth, for the Old Testament Law required a brother to marry his widowed sister-in-law if he were free to do so in order that the family name might be carried on. Then the Sadducees popped the question: "In the resurrection therefore, . . . whose wife shall she be of them? For the seven had her to wife" (Mark 12:23).

I can just see them with self-satisfied smirks on their faces waiting for the Lord to try to answer that one. Well, He did—by reminding them that they were just plain ignorant of the Scriptures which they thought they knew and had even used in their illustration. He said in effect, "The Scriptures say that marriage is of no concern in the resurrection life, and therefore your question needs no answer. If you had known as much about the resurrection life as you professed to know about the Law of Moses, you would not have asked the question." The whole question was out of order because it was an ignorant question.

In Romans 9 we have a scriptural example of an impertinent question. You recall that in this chapter Paul is discussing the very difficult and intricate subject of the sovereignty of God. He points out the fact that in one instance God made a choice between two children even before they were born in order that His purpose according to election might stand on the obvious basis of God's calling alone and not of works (v. 11). At this point Paul lets an imaginary critic ask two questions. The first one in verse

14 is this: If God chooses on this basis, is He not unrighteous? The answer is a resounding no. If God acted only according to pure righteousness, everyone would be condemned. God is also merciful and shows that mercy to whomever He wishes. This raises the second question in verse 19: Then why does God find fault with what I do? If everything is in His will, then even if I sin I have not resisted His will. Paul's reply to this is simply that it is an impertinent question. He says: "Nay but, O man, who art thou that repliest against God? Shall the thing formed say to him that formed it, Why hast thou made me thus? Hath not the potter power over the clay, of the same lump to make one vessel unto honour, and another unto dishonour?" (vv. 20-21).

I remember seeing this once. A young boy was sitting at a potter's wheel making little vases. Over in the corner of the shop was a large mound of clay. As soon as I came along, he grabbed a chunk of clay and slapped it on the wheel, which he moved with his feet, and he rather quickly fashioned a little vase. It was all finished and he was taking it off the wheel by pulling a tightly stretched fine wire under the base of it while it was still turning on the wheel. Only, just as he was doing that, one side of the vase collapsed. But that didn't faze him. He simply took the ruined vase, threw it in the corner, took another chunk of clay, slapped it on the wheel, shaped it, took it off with the fine wire, and proudly held up a perfect vase for me to see. Now wouldn't it be silly to think of that piece of clay standing up and saying, "You can't do this to me. I have rights! I'm a fine piece of clay." "O man, who art thou that repliest against God?"

May I also point out to you some ignorant and impertinent questions which are sometimes asked in theology? We make fun of the ancient scholastics who spent their time discussing how many angels could stand on the point of a pin, and yet even today we get similarly foolish questions.

Sometimes these question are on the doctrine of the sovereignty of God. For instance: What would have happened if Adam hadn't sinned? This is an ignorant question because it shows ignorance of the meaning of the Scripture that tells us that the Lamb of God was foreordained before the foundation of the world (1 Pet 1:20). But if you insist on an answer to the question, it is simply this: If Adam had not sinned, then there would have been a different plan of God. But it would have been a different preplanned plan, not a plan put into effect after God saw whether Adam would sin or not.

Here's another: Can a nonelect person believe? Or will an elect person refuse to believe? These are impertinent questions which place man in the position of replying against God. What you need to remember is that God has a plan including an elect people, and that at the same time, and without contradiction, God, through your witnessing, offers His grace freely to all.

Eschatology is another area from which these questions arise. For instance: If the Jews had accepted the Kingdom offered by Christ, would there have been any place or necessity for the cross? This is an ignorant question, yet it is commonly asked by those who are not premillennialists. Certainly premillennialism teaches that the Lord offered a Kingdom to the Jews which was postponed because of their refusal to accept it, but it is not true that had they accepted the Kingdom there would have been no cross.

The cross was necessary in any case, for the Kingdom as well as the Church is built on the suffering Messiah.

Or again, here's a question which posttribulationists ask in order to try to embarrass pretribulationists: If you believe that the Church will be raptured before the Tribulation, then there will not be enough time for God to judge all the saints in seven short years before the second coming of Christ. It is estimated that there are two hundred million living Christians. In seven years there are just over two hundred million seconds. So each judgment could last only one second, and that's not enough time. So the pretribulation rapture view is wrong, they say. Slightly impertinent, isn't it, to limit God in such a way?

Now, having cited these examples from the Scriptures and from theology, may I cite a few from you. These are things I hear. Or I see them enacted in lives, whether I hear them from lips or not. Here's the first: "Why isn't it all right if I fool around? It's my life." Answer: The fruit of the Spirit is self-control, not fooling around. And you are not your own, but your life has been bought with a price.

Here's another: "Everything is a part of God's will. So if I fail a test, God can't blame me because I've just done His will." Sounds like that imaginary questioner whom Paul put in his place twenty centuries ago in Romans 9. Answer: It is required of students, I mean stewards, that a man be found faithful—not flunking.

Or another: "What difference does it make whether or not I prayed this morning?" Answer: "Men ought always to pray, and not to faint" (Luke 18:1).

Or: "If I drop out of school and get married, so what?" Answer: "I say therefore to the unmarried and widows, It is good for them if they abide even as I. The time is short: it

61

remaineth, that . . . they that have wives be as though they had none" (1 Cor 7:8, 29). And if the time was short in Paul's day, it's ever shorter today.

What's the moral of all this? Simply this: Don't waste your precious time worrying about foolish questions. The plan to follow is to concentrate on what you do understand, seek to obey God in that, and leave the unanswered and the future in His hands. There's just one question you ought to be concentrating on every day. It's important today. It will be important tomorrow, and the day after. It is simply this: "Am I doing the will of God as best I know it right now?"

# 10

## Giving God's Way

WITHOUT APOLOGY the New Testament places a great deal of emphasis on the subject of giving. There are commands, practical suggestions, warnings, examples, and exhortations concerning this important matter. Everywhere in the Scriptures miserliness, greed, and avarice are denounced; and generosity, hospitality, and charity extolled. The same word used for our fellowship with the Lord is also used in relation to the fellowship of the giving of money (2 Cor 8:4), emphasizing the high spiritual character of giving. Further, this grace of giving is a spiritual gift (Rom 12:8) available to all believers to have and to use. It is a gift which all can exercise, whatever the individual's financial status, and it is one of high order among the believer's total privileges and responsibilities.

What should be one's guide in grace giving? Perhaps the New Testament passage which sets forth most succinctly the basic principles of giving is 1 Corinthians 16:2: "Upon the first day of the week let every one of you lay by him in store, as God hath prospered him, that there be no gatherings when I come." In this single verse there are laid down four principles for enjoying the grace of giving:

1. Giving is incumbent on each person—"let every one of you." Grace does not make giving optional; it is the privilege and responsibility of every Christian. Therefore, when you or I fail to give, the entire Church is weakened, for, like the proverbial chain, the Church is no better than its weakest member. Nevertheless, giving is a personal matter in which every believer sustains a direct and individual responsibility to the Lord as if he were the only Christian in the world. What you give is your personal business as long as you are giving and doing it in conference with Him before whom all things are naked and open.

2. Giving is to be proportionate—"as God hath prospered him." No hard and fast rule concerning the amount is to be found among New Testament principles of giving. This is in sharp contrast to the Old Testament regulations, which required that a tenth of all be given to the Levites (Lev 27:30-33), who in turn tithed what they received and gave it to the priests. In addition, the Jews apparently understood that a second tithe (a tenth of the remaining nine-tenths) was to be set apart and consumed in a sacred meal in Jerusalem. (Those living too far from Jerusalem could bring money, Deut 12:5-6, 11, 18.) Further, every third year another tithe was taken for the Levites, strangers, fatherless, and widows (Deut 14:28-29). Thus, the proportion was clearly specified, and every Israelite was obligated to bring to the Lord approximately 22 percent of his yearly income. In contrast, the New Testament merely says, "as God hath prospered him." This may mean 8, 12, 20, or 50 percent, or even more, depending on the indi-

vidual case. It will also undoubtedly mean variation in proportion, for there is no reason to believe that the proportion suitable for this year will be satisfactory for next year. When prosperity comes, as it has for many Christians, it should be used to give more, not necessarily to buy more. Each time the Christian gives he is to reflect on God's blessing in his life and determine what proportion in return he will give to God.

3. Giving is to be in private deposit—"lay by him in store." Contrary to the usual belief, the Christian is not told to turn his gift into the church treasury each Sunday. The phrase "in store" means "to gather and lay up, to heap up or treasure"; and the reflexive pronoun form "to himself" indicates that it is to be kept in private, not public, deposit. The picture clearly set forth in this phrase is of a private gift fund into which the believer places his proportionately determined gifts and out of which he distributes to specific needs. This does not mean that either the giving into such a fund or the paying out from such a fund is spasmodic. Neither does this mean that regular giving or even pledging is contrary to the New Testament principles of giving (cf. 2 Cor 8:10-11, where a pledge was made). But it does mean that there should be, however small, an ever ready supply of money available to give out as the Spirit directs, both regularly and occasionally.

4. Giving should be planned—"upon the first day of the week." It has already been suggested that this is not an erratic business. The laying by in private store should be done on Sunday. Sunday is the God-appointed day to keep accounts, determine proportions, and lay by in store. The Scriptures do not say much about what the Christian should or should not do on the Lord's Day except that he

65

should assemble with other believers (Heb 10:25) and do his giving (1 Cor 16:2). Though one need not become ritualistic about this matter of caring for financial matters on Sunday, one must not treat it lightly either. Here is a God-given exhortation which might well be heeded. The writer has himself made a practice in the past few years, whenever possible, of setting aside on Sunday the proportion of his income which will go to the Lord's work, and, strange as it may seem, doing it on the Lord's Day seems to bring an added blessing. One of my students tried this last year and testified to the blessing it brought to his family; for, gathered together as a family group on Sunday afternoon, thinking and praying together about their giving to the Lord, their spiritual ties were strengthened. If God has suggested it, it is certainly worth trying.

"But," someone may say, "why go to all this trouble? Why not just tithe?" The word *tithe* is found in the New Testament only eight times (Matt 23:23; Luke 11:42; 18:12; Heb 7:5-6, 8-9). In the references in the gospels it is used in connection with what the Pharisees were doing in fulfilling their obligation to the Mosaic Law. In the references in Hebrews it is used to prove the inferiority of the tribe of Levi, to whom the tithe was given. There is no passage of Scripture that enjoins, either by direct command or example, the tithe upon the believer in this age. It is apparent that the tithe was part of the Mosaic Law (Lev 27:30-33) and an important factor in the economy of Israel. The Law was never given to Gentiles and is expressly done away for the Christian (Rom 2:14; 2 Cor 3:7-13; Heb 7:11-12, 18). Further, it would be impossible today to tithe as commanded in the Old Testament, for where is the priesthood to whom tithes could be paid? Neither are the words of

Malachi 3 for the Christian, for what believer claims to be a son of Jacob, to whom the passage is addressed (v. 6)? Material abundance is never promised today as a reward for faithfulness in any area of living, including giving. God promises spiritual blessing (Eph 1:3) and the meeting of material needs (Phil 4:19). Being prospered materially is not sign of deep godliness or faithful tithing, and, contrariwise, poverty is no indication of being out of God's will (cf. Paul's own case in Phil 4:12).

But, it may be asked, since tithing was practiced before the Law, does that not make irrelevant all that has been said above and leave tithing as a proper principle for giving? Since Abraham and Jacob both tithed, and since their acts antedated the Law, does that not relieve tithing of its legal aspects and make it a valid principle to follow today? The answer would be yes if there were no other guides for giving in the New Testament. Since there are such standards in the New Testament, why go back to two isolated examples in the Old Testament to find the principles for giving? The fact that something was done before the Law which was later incorporated into the Law does not necessarily make that thing a good example for today, especially if the New Testament gives further guidance on the matter. Not even the most ardent tither would say that the Sabbath should be observed today because it was observed before the Law (Exod 16:23-36), and yet that is the very reasoning used in promoting tithing. The New Testament teaches us about a new day of worship, and it also gives us new directions for giving. To tithe today on the basis of the examples of those who did it before the Law would mean that only 10 percent of one's income would go to the Lord and possibly only occasionally (as in the example of Abraham); to bring the tithes commanded by the Law would mean paying more than 10 percent, and it would also mean that it should be given to support Judaism; to give on the basis of the principles of the New Testament might mean any percent given, because 100 percent already belongs to Him. The Lord's work will never lack support if we preach and practice New Testament principles of giving.

Proportionate giving is not starting with a tithe and then doing what more we can when we can. Proportionate giving is as God has prospered. Rather, a large income means a large proportion; a smaller income, a smaller proportion. If someone felt after prayer that his proportion should be around 10 percent, the writer would suggest that he give 9 percent or 11 percent just to keep his thinking out of the 10 percent rut. A man who is giving 9 percent or 11 percent will find it much easier to change his proportion than the Christian who confines himself to 10 percent.

This is in no way a doctrine of lawlessness. Though we are not under the Law, we are in-lawed to Christ, and this assures proper conduct in all areas of life, including that of giving. When I say, as I do, "I do not tithe," I am not saying, "I do not give." Every Christian owes 100 percent of what he is and what he has to God, and I for one have willingly given all to Him. The question, then, is not only "How much do I give?" but also "How much do I spend on myself?" Proportionate giving alone can furnish the right answer to this problem. "Charge them that are rich in this world, that they be not highminded, nor trust in uncertain riches, but in the living God, who giveth us richly all things to enjoy; that they do good, that they be rich in good works, ready to distribute, willing to communicate; laying up in store for themselves a good foundation against the time to come, that they may lay hold on eternal life" (1 Tim 6:17-19). We give because he gave, not because he commanded; we give because we want to, not because we have to. If in turn He blesses materially, we praise Him; if not, we still praise Him. This is grace giving.

# 11

## *Led of the Lord*

I ALWAYS HESITATE to talk about the leading of the Lord. As soon as I do, the Lord always brings something into my own life which requires me to find His will. And then I look back on all my wonderful messages on how to know the will of God and wonder if they were of any use to anybody. But in spite of the risk involved, I am going to discuss how to know the will of God.

We're going to look at this subject from an Old Testament passage. I realize that we do not build a doctrine on a picture, but nevertheless this particular picture in Numbers 9 points out the principal matters which should concern us about the leading of the Lord. Will you look at Numbers 9:15-23.

From this picture of life in the camp of Israel I want to point out several things that are extremely pertinent to determining the leading of the Lord for your life.

The first one is this: *The leading of the Lord is based on a fundamental certainty.* It is not based on peripheral things, not on minor things, not on feelings, not on circumstances, not on friends, not on fleeces, but on the certainty of the presence of the Lord. When any Israelite wanted to know where he should be, he looked at that which signified the presence of the Lord in the camp—the cloud and the fire. When God's presence led him on, he moved. When His presence stayed, he stayed. God gave Israel this certain guide—His own presence. And God has given the Christian the same guide—His own presence living in your life.

I admit it would be much easier to have a nice little formula we could use in determining God's will. To be able to use a set of rules or some simple test would be quite convenient. But these things are *not* the means of discovering God's leading. The leading of the Lord is known by you personally simply by being in fellowship with the Lord. You ask Him, and you receive the answer from Him. It is based on the certainty of His presence in your heart and life.

Now, this means that knowing the will of God is *not* based on the many other things which many of us use. One is the fleece. The chief trouble with the fleece is simply that it limits God's leading to two ways. There are only two choices with a fleece, and usually those two are things you have thought of. Perhaps God has in mind several other possibilities which you have not considered. A fleece will not reveal them. I am afraid that a fleece is often a cheap substitute for real communion with God that enables you to receive your leading from Him directly. I will say, however, that after you have the mind of the Lord it is often useful and quite proper to ask Him to confirm your leading in some way. But determination and confirmation are two different things, and the determination of God's will should be on the basis of communion with Him.

In seminary days I lived near a fellow who was a senior. I, being a freshman and very impressionable, thought if anybody knew anything about the leading of the Lord a senior would. I happened into his room one night when he had apparently just finished praying. But on his bed were five slips of paper. I said, "What are you doing?" He replied, "I'm trying to find out what I ought to do when I graduate. So I've written five choices on these slips of paper, and I've just finished asking the Lord to help me choose the right one. Now I'm going to pick a piece of paper, and that will be the Lord's will for me!" At least this was not limiting the will of God to two choices!

God's will is not based on circumstances, either. So often you hear Christians say, "Well, it's an open door, so it must be God's will for me." But don't you realize that Satan can open and shut doors of opportunity too?

Friends also can be either a help or a hindrance. Seek their advice but not their leading. The facts may come through friends, but the leading must come from the Lord to you directly. You see, there can be no substitute for genuine, unbroken fellowship with Him, for this is the basic, the certainty in God's leading.

The second thing to notice about this story is this: *The leading of the Lord is clear.* For the Israelites, it wasn't confused, it wasn't hazy, it wasn't obscure; it was perfectly clear. An Israelite knew exactly where the Lord wanted him. And furthermore, God's leading was clear to all in the camp. Moses didn't have some inside track to God. Everyone could see when it was time to move and when it was time to stay.

I am not contradicting what I have just said about friends, but, if you have the leading of God, some others at least will recognize it. It is not that friends guide you, but they will recognize that you have the mind of the Lord. If

72

nobody else thinks you are right, then be careful. You ought to begin to reexamine what you thought to be God's will. After all, there are other spiritually minded people in the world besides yourself, who, although it is not their leading, are in a position of fellowship with Christ so that they can discern the facts in your case. It is especially important for young people to remember that older people do have some wisdom and might well be consulted! The whole camp of Israel clearly knew what God's will was. Don't wander off into the desert alone. Don't think you have an inside track to God—some sort of direct pipeline to the Almighty—especially when no one else sees it as you do.

Notice, too, that God's will was always clear. Whether it was day or night, the Israelites knew the will of God. And if you are in fellowship with the Lord, you always will know His will. But it all depends on fellowship with Him.

Both the steps and the stops were ordered of the Lord. Just because they were asked to remain in a certain place for a while did not mean that they were out of God's will. Sometimes we get the idea that we need the leading of the Lord only for the extra special matter like a summer job, or a place of ministry after graduation, or where to go to school. You need to know His will all the time, and it will be plain in the stops as well as the steps. For instance, if God leads you to school, then generally He leads you to stay in that school until you graduate. If so, that means you are in God's will today in school, and you should be zealous to fulfill His will in your studies, your jobs, your sports, your social life, in everything. It is just as important to fulfill His will where the cloud is resting today as when it moves to a summer or postgraduation job.

Now there is a third thing about this picture: *God's leading is conditioned.* It is conditioned on your choosing to want to have His will for your life. I'm afraid that even in Christian schools there are those who have never made that basic choice. They haven't decided whose will they will follow in their lives. They are still dabbling and compromising, having never said, "Lord, I take Your will for my life." There must be this basic decision first.

Then there must be constant fellowship with the Lord. Just because you have given your life to the Lord doesn't mean that you will not ever sin again. But when sin comes, then there has to be confession on the basis of 1 John 1:9. In other words, and in accordance with our picture from the Old Testament, you have to keep your eyes constantly on the cloud.

Finally, there must be obedience to what has already been revealed to you. You must not expect God to reveal further steps to you unless you have taken the first steps. If you refuse the first, don't be surprised if you never learn the second. Constant obedience is indispensable.

Don't come up to your senior year and then ask the Lord for guidance in an act of desperation. Now is the time, freshmen, to fulfill all of the will of God—in school. If you haven't made a good scholastic record during all four years, don't blame the registrar if he can't send a good transcript to the graduate school you want to enter. And don't blame the Lord. Be obedient to today's assignments, and you will not put any limitation on God's leading tomorrow.

# 12

## *"I Don't Need to Know Anything but the Bible"*

WHENEVER MY WIFE THINKS I am being just a little hypocritical about something, she smiles sweetly and says, "Why, you pious fraud!" Her serious joke usually brings me up short because there is nothing quite so pathetically humorous as someone who is trying to fake piety. Let me introduce you to a typical pious fraud.

He is the student who says, "I don't need to know anything but the Bible." Sometimes you find this kind of fraud in Bible schools. Or he may say, "I'd rather know the Bible and not know anything else than to know everything else and not know the Bible." Now, of course, there is some truth in any fraud, especially a pious one! And it is certainly true that if you have to choose between secular knowledge and Bible knowledge, the latter is greatly to be preferred. But who says you have to choose?

Another variation goes like this: "What good are all these secular subjects? I came to Bible school to learn the Bible. I don't need to study English, literature, science, accounting, and all that useless stuff. I'm called to preach. All I need to know is the Bible."

Or sometimes I hear it put this way: "Liberal arts in a Bible college! I can't see the use of such courses. However, I guess they are necessary evils, so I'll just pass them and really concentrate on Bible. That's what I came for." Of course, the students who are barely skinning through their liberal arts courses are always getting all A's in their Bible courses, are they not?

Now, there are some very fine arguments put forward to support this pious fraud. Since I want to be very pious myself, I am going to argue in favor of this idea! I have cataloged the arguments in favor of this under two headings.

First, there are some scriptural arguments for not studying anything but the Bible. Here is one: "Hath not God made foolish the wisdom of this world?" (1 Cor 1:20). The "wisdom of this world" certainly must include English, literature, science, and accounting, and any other secular subject I do not happen to like! Here is another one: "But the natural man receiveth not the things of the Spirit of God: for they are foolishness unto him: neither can he know them, because they are spiritually discerned" (1 Cor 2:14). Or how about this? "But what things were gain to me, those I counted loss for Christ. Yea doubtless, and I count all things but loss for the excellency of the knowledge of Christ Jesus my Lord" (Phil 3:7-8). Those are pretty good verses, are they not, especially if you want to call useless some secular subject you are not passing.

Second, there is the logical argument. It goes like this: "I don't see any use in these courses, so why bother with them?" The courses are not useful, so, *ergo,* they aren't necessary! Good old **American** pragmatism has crept into our sacred Bible school atmosphere. But look at the argument. "*I* don't see any use." Ah, there is the error. Are you so capable a judge as to be able to discern the importance or nonimportance of everything in this world? But you say you are not talking about everything in this world, just about English literature. But are you so omniscient that you can see all the ramifications and possibilities of future usefulness of English literature that you can discard it as umimportant? So what, that *you* do not see any use in something? Who are you? Just because you say it is not useful, does that make it worthless and everybody else wrong who sees some use in it?

"Well," you say, "maybe there is some use in it, but not for me, and since I don't intend to use the knowledge of these courses, I don't see any use in taking them." Well, there are a lot of things in life which do not seem to be of any use personally, but which, if you stop and think about them a minute, are useful in some way or another. There is not much practical use in just sitting and watching a sunset as far as I can see. After all, I am not an artist and I cannot paint a picture of that sunset and then sell it for useful money. But you say it does something for your soul. When you're so very busy it does you good to sit still and watch a sunset. You find it useful to meditate for those few moments. And you are right. There is use in a lot of things even though we do not see it immediately.

What most of us really mean when we say something is not useful is that we do not find any pleasure in it. If you do not happen to be the contemplative type I could argue all day with you about the usefulness of watching a sunset, but you would never really be convinced. If something does not seem to be useful to me, and in addition I do not enjoy doing it, then I am convinced it is not useful. If I enjoy, it, even though it does not seem to be useful, then usually I will find some way to justify its usefulness. But if I neither see the usefulness nor enjoy the experience, I write it off as useless. This is the case with those secular courses you do not like. But if you did happen to like one of them, you would not call it useless, even though you did not see any purpose in it for you. A lot of you spend a great deal of time uselessly watching the world series on TV. But what use is that? You cannot even cheer your team on, since you are not in the park. The only use is the pleasure you receive; and watching a world series is certainly legitimate recreation. But some of you girls who do not happen to enjoy baseball cannot see any use at all in watching it.

The real reason for this fraud is laziness. It is a lot easier to speak with authority about the Bible whether you have ever taken a Bible course or not. But if you do not speak English correctly or you cannot conjugate a French verb or recite a poem accurately or keep books, then all can see your ignorance. It is a pious fraud to cry, "I'd rather know the Bible than anything; away with all these useless secular courses," because you can more easily fake your knowledge of the Bible than you can cover up your ignorance of other things.

Let us look at some fallacies in this fraud. First, it is illogical. It is illogical to say you do not need to know anything but what is in the Bible. Do not forget, although the Bible is truth, not all the truth is in the Bible. There are a lot of things—true things—which God has not revealed in His Word. If all you need to know is in the Bible, then you fellows had better quit driving your cars, and you girls should give up fixing your hair, because the subjects of driving and cosmetology are secular, not biblical. Also, we can all eat anything we want anytime, because the Bible does not teach us about dietetics. Oh, you say that is ridiculous. It is just as ridiculous as your saying you do not need to know literature or science or math because it is not in the Bible. Even the Bible itself recognizes that there is truth which it does not contain. When children are commanded to obey their parents, the Bible is saying that the parents will teach and lead children into specifics which are not in the Bible.

Second, this pious fraud is unscriptural. The Bible itself includes many examples of men who knew the wisdom of this world, and makes many allusions to secular subjects. While we recognize that the biblical revelation is not mainly concerned with secular knowledge, all these glimpses we do have of secular wisdom in its pages should alert any pious fraud to the fact that men of the Bible were educated in fields other than the sacred. May I remind you of Abraham the businessman. Or remember Moses who studied the wisdom of Egypt—and he was not out of the will of God in doing so. Or think of Daniel spending those three long years in the king's school in Babylon learning science and a foreign language.

There are many allusions to secular subjects in the pages of Scripture. Many of the references are incidental, and we would expect them to be so. But the simple fact that they are there ought to squelch this fraud once for all. Physical science was known in the time of Job (Job 9:9) and Isaiah (Isa 13:10). Paul was acquainted with the schools of philosophic thought of his day as evinced by his reference to the Stoics and Epicureans on Mars' Hill. Paul spoke a foreign language, for when he spoke in his own defense at the Temple in Jerusalem the people were amazed to hear him address them in Aramaic (Acts 22:2). You see, he was a Hellenistic Jew and would have known Greek as his native tongue, but he also knew Hebrew. Furthermore, the Greek he knew, he knew well. When he stood in his defense again before King Agrippa and Queen Bernice, he spoke very cultured Greek (cf. Acts 26:4 where Paul uses the very polite form of "know"). What a student of history Stephen was! Of course, it was not U. S. history, but it was his native history (Acts 7). At least three times Paul shows his acquaintance with heathen literature; and while that does not make him a specialist, it does show that he knew subjects that were not in the Bible (Acts 17:28; 1 Cor 15:33; Titus 1:12). Paul uses applied psychology in that Titus passage, for having cited the fact that the Cretians were liars, evil beasts, and gluttons, he tells Titus to use sharp rebuke with such people. And need I speak of medicine when Luke's writings are filled with medical terms? Astronomy, philosophy, foreign language, grammar, history, literature, psychology, and medicine—that is quite a list.

What I am saying is simply this: it is not a question of whether you should know the Bible and nothing else or whether you should know everything else and not the Bible. It is not either or. There is a third choice. You can know the Bible *and* these other things. It is far better to be an educated saint than a pious fraud.

We have come to that time when some of you are going to have to think very clearly about priorities. The pressure of studies has begun to catch up with you. Don't hide behind some pious-sounding statement. If the Lord led you to school or college, He led you to master the variety of subjects which the curriculum sets before you. It is up to you to decide just what you are going to give your first attention to. Do not let the genuine decisions which you made at the beginning of the school year deteriorate into pious platitudes. Make it your ambition to be as fully trained as you possibly can so that the Lord who has called you will be able to use you to the fullest in the years to come.

# 13

## *"I'm too Spiritual to Have Fun"*

I SUPPOSE that all the brains were very happy with the last chapter, while the fun boys squirmed. Well, fasten your seat belts, because we are going to turn the tables. I want to talk to you about the pious fraud of saying, "I'm too spiritual to have fun." It is the misconception that piety and fun cannot be mixed. And by fun I mean socializing, parties, sports, and so forth.

Sometimes the fraud is stated in a form of logic. It goes like this: "Parties are worldly; I certainly do not want to be worldly; therefore, I will not go to parties."

But the ultimate in stating this fraud is this: "I don't believe it's spiritual to waste money on such frivolities. A Christian should certainly be careful with his money, and any dollar spent on a party could be put to much better use, so naturally since I'm spiritually minded I won't spend any of my money on parties." However, it has been my observation that such people do not put their party money in the offering or give it to missions; they usually find some other way to spend it on themselves.

Of course, there are some arguments that can be advanced in support of this, and I want to remind you of them and then try to help you see them in proper perspective.

The first is the priority argument. If you give proper priority to studies, as I have suggested, there will not be time for all this partying and socializing I am talking about now. But there is really no contradiction. A priority list is a list, and while there is one thing at the top of the list—the item with highest priority—there are also other things on the list. There wll be a number of things on your priority list. So there is no contradiction between saying that your training—meaning your studies and service— are to be given top priority and that there will be other things on your list. However, I want to reiterate that I do not believe there ought to be any question in your minds that your preparation in studies and practical service are top priority during these years in school. But these things are not your whole diet. That list will contain things in slots three, four, and five for your well-rounded life. Thus the priority argument must be seen in the perspective of a priority list.

The second argument concerns the use of money. I alluded to it a moment ago when I said some argue that spending money on parties is frivolity, not spirituality. Now, don't misunderstand me. As Christians we need to be particularly careful of how we spend our money. All we possess is from God, and all we spend ought to be directed by Him. Every penny that comes into your possession ought to be very carefully and wisely used. May I just make two observations about this? It's the worst kind of pious fraud to say you won't spend money on a date or party or recreation when you will feed your face with unnecessary food between every class and every night, when you just

83

have to "go out." "Oh," you say, "that's different. Food is for my body, and that's necessary." But dates are for your soul, and some of you need your souls stirred up once in a while by a good date or party!

The second observation about this false financial argument is this. Do you remember the incident recorded in Matthew 26:6-13? It's about Mary who anointed the Lord's feet with a very costly ointment. Do you remember the reaction of the pious disciples? They were indignant and said, "To what purpose is this waste? For this ointment might have been sold for much and given to the poor." Our version might be, "Why should we have a school banquet? The money could be given to missions and used much more profitably." But recall the Lord's reply: "For ye have the poor always with you; but me ye have not always." Of course, I'm not suggesting that everything we do socially is in the same category as what this woman did to Christ, but I am suggesting that sometimes we are not really capable of judging accurately what is really waste and what is really useful. Even the disciples who had walked with Him for more than three years misjudged the real value of this seeming waste of money which might have—in their estimation—been more profitably given to the poor.

Besides these arguments from priorities and finances, I suppose there are some scriptural arguments to support this fraud, but honestly, I have difficulty finding them. Perhaps you could use such a verse as "Let your moderation be known unto all men. The Lord is at hand" (Phil 4:5), or "Be sober, be vigilant" (1 Pet 5:8), and you certainly cannot do that at a party. I expect most of us, rather than being able to point to specific Scriptures, think the general tone of the Bible and the example of the life of Christ support this idea. We think of our Lord in His times of early morning prayer and communion, or in His moments of agonizing prayer, or in His constant witnessing, and we conclude that since socializing had no place in His life, having fun can't be spiritual.

But what are the real reasons for our thinking this way? This is a hard question, but let me suggest two things. First, many young people of your age are just plain shy, and it's simply hard for them to date or mix socially with others. May I say that I have a great deal of sympathy for them, and I suggest that all of us ought to help one another in this regard. And it doesn't help to broadcast the fact that a couple is going steady because they've had two dates together. The only way to overcome shyness is to make yourself participate in social life, and the best time to start is now. Second, I am inclined to think that some people—especially fellows—are lazy to the point of not wanting to make the effort to get dressed up and put on good manners for a date. It is much easier to be slovenly than to be a lady or a gentleman. The escapist counterculture proves that. It's just easier to be your sloppy old self.

Having said all this, I finally come to the text for this chapter. I want you to open your Bible and look at it, because if you don't, you won't believe it's there. It's Matthew 11:19: "The Son of man came eating and drinking." Did you know that was in the Bible? "Oh, yes," you say, "but I thought it was sarcasm, not a fact." It is sarcasm to some extent, but it is also a factual characterization of the life of Christ. You see, the contrast is between John the Baptist and the Lord. John was an ascetic and did not participate in social affairs. But the people did not receive him; instead, they said he was demon-possessed. In contrast, the Lord came eating and drinking, but the people did not receive Him either. Instead, they said He was "gluttonous, and a winebibber." The Lord said to the people, "What do you want? John gave you the opportunity to mourn with him, and I have given you the opportunity to rejoice with Me. You wouldn't accept either of us, though our ministries are characterized by exact opposites." But in so characterizing these ministries, the Lord said His own was that of one who came eating and drinking.

Before you begin to think I am way off base, may I remind you of a few incidents. Under what circumstances was the first miracle performed? At a wedding feast. This festive social occasion was Jesus' choice for manifesting His glory to His disciples (John 2:11). I once read a very startling comment on this passage. It went something like this: It's harder to go to a party and behave like the Son of God than it is to stay home and pray. And often it is!

Do you remember what happened after Matthew was converted? He did a most natural thing. He invited his friends to meet the Master. Only, his friends were publicans and sinners, and nice religious people just didn't associate with such. So when the Pharisees found out about it, they accused the Lord, who promptly rebuked them for not realizing that such people needed to be reached (Matt 9:10-13). And if they can be reached at a dinner party, then let's reach them there.

Do you remember under what circumstances Peter's mother-in-law was healed? The Lord had gone to Peter's house after a synagogue service. Finding her sick, He healed her, and then they all had a festive meal (Matt

8:14-15). On another occasion the Lord Jesus went to a chief Pharisee's house to eat a Sabbath meal and to witness to the people gathered there (Luke 14:1-6). For all the restrictions on the Sabbath day, we should not forget that the meal on that day was a very festive occasion— prepared ahead of time, of course, in order not to break the laws concerning cooking on the Sabbath. It was on this occasion in that chief Pharisee's house that the Lord gave a very interesting parable (Luke 14:12-14). In essence, He said this: "When you plan a big dinner, don't invite those who are sure to invite you to their house later. Rather, invite folks who cannot possibly repay you, because this is true hospitality." You see, the Lord is saying that being sociable is not the same as socializing as we commonly see it practiced today.

Finally, do you remember the dinner which the Lord attended after the resurrection of Lazarus (John 12:1-11)? It was on this occasion that Mary anointed His feet with the costly ointment. There is no record in the gospels of any occasion when Christ refused an invitation like those connected with these five incidents I have just cited. Even the Lord's Supper was a meal, and certainly the marriage feast of the Lamb will be a festive occasion. The Son of Man indeed came eating and drinking. But scandalized sanctimoniousness says, "You mustn't do such things because it isn't spiritual."

Before I conclude, I want to be sure we keep a proper balance about this whole idea by pointing out three dangers. The first is overindulgence. Almost anything good that God has given us can be perverted by overuse. Think, for instance, of the miracle of the feeding of the five thousand. If there had been too much food, the people would have been involved in gluttony. Most good things can be misused by overuse. People who are always partying or playing are just as wrong as people who are never doing these things.

Second, beware of wrong motivation in your social life. There's nothing worse than Christian social ladder climbing. Wherever you go or whatever you do, it should be to promote your Lord, not yourself.

Third, beware of a wrong aim. I am certainly not suggesting it is wrong to enjoy yourself. It isn't. But it is wrong if in the enjoyment Christ is not also manifested as He was at Cana. You should go, participate, have fun, enjoy yourself, and show off Christ, all at the same time. I do not mean that we have the fun part of an evening and then suddenly shift gears, quiet down, and have "devotions." I mean that both in the fun and in the quiet we exhibit Him.

And now, finally, here's a second text with which I close the chapter. It's 1 Corinthians 10:31, which does not say, "Whether therefore ye read your Bible, or pray, or whatsoever ye do, do all to the glory of God." It does say, "Whether therefore ye eat, or drink, or whatsoever ye do, do all to the glory of God." It is a lot easier to show the glory of God in a prayer meeting than in the cafeteria line. Don't hide behind a false piety which says, "I'm too spiritual to have fun." The Son of Man came eating and drinking; therefore, whether you eat or drink, do all to the glory of God.

# 14

## "I Don't Need Anyone to Teach Me the Bible"

HERE IS ANOTHER FRAUD. It is pious like the others, and because of that, there is some truth in it. But it is not the whole truth, and that makes it a fraud. It goes like this: "I don't need anyone to teach me the Bible." Sometimes it is stated this way: "I don't want to be known as a man of books; I want to be known as a man of *the* Book." Or often I hear it expressed just a little differently. We are told it is not necessary to know what other people say about the Bible. All we need is what the Lord gives us directly from the Bible. "Don't listen to what men say; learn from the Lord directly." Among students, this same pious fraud provides an interesting excuse when writing certain term papers. It is used like this: "Why do I need a bibliography in a Bible paper? If I quote the Bible, isn't that enough? To quote mere men would be serving no purpose. The idea of that teacher requiring a bibliography!"

This fraud can lead to several serious errors. The first is ignorance. If we hide under the skirts of this fraud too long, we will never progress in our knowledge of the Bible. But you say, "Other men have been well taught by the Lord and without the benefit of formal education." That is true, but these men studied, and they studied the writings of the sages in order to be well taught. Of course, they had to be given understanding by the Holy Spirit, but the Spirit often teaches us through the works of other men. Too much of this fraud will lead to nothing but profound ignorance of the Word, not knowledge of it.

Second, it can lead to a false kind of meditative mysticism. Do you know what I mean? I mean the kind of thing where you sit down in the morning, open the Bible at random, are "given" a verse, and then run wild on the meaning of it. You really do not understand what that verse means, but you hypnotize yourself into thinking it has some special or deep meaning to you personally. Now, do not misunderstand me. I hope the Lord does speak to your heart each day through His Word. But be sure that what He says is truly based on the precise meaning of that verse and not on what you may think it means or what you may want it to mean.

Third, this meditatively mystical interpretation of the Bible easily leads to a false leading of the Lord in the decisions of your life. It is very easy to pass from a mystical meditation ungoverned by knowledge to saying, "The Lord led me to do such and such," and then to justify that action on the basis of your ignorance of the Word. It is a wishful leading, not a spiritual leading.

Does the fraud have any support? Certainly, because there is some truth in it. In John 16:13 the Lord said: "Howbeit when he, the Spirit of truth, is come, he will guide you into all truth: for he shall not speak of himself;

but whatsoever he shall hear, that shall he speak: and he will shew you things to come." Paul reminds us in 1 Corinthians 2:12 that "we have received, not the spirit of the world, but the spirit which is of God; that we might know the things that are freely given to us of God." Now, there is very important truth in these passages. Again I emphasize that it is easy to be misunderstood in talking about these frauds, simply because the statement of the fraud is neither wholly correct nor entirely wrong. The ministry of the Holy Spirit in your life in teaching you the truth of God is indispensable. But these passages do not teach us that this ministry of the Spirit is always direct. Nothing is said about the means He may use to teach us. It may be direct, as you quietly and persistently think about a passage, but it may be through intermediate means. And some of these intermediate means are the books of men—both living and dead, teachers, chapels, concordances, and many more things.

If God does not teach us through teachers, for instance, then please tell me what purpose He had in giving the gift of teaching to the Church. This gift, you remember, is mentioned in all three passages on gifts in the New Testament. But if the Holy Spirit is always going to teach you directly without any intermediate means, then there would be no need for the gift of teaching. You must have the Spirit's ministry if you are to learn the Bible, but there is nothing in the Bible that says His ministry may not come through men or books.

Since this fraud might be more easily misunderstood than some of the others, I want to talk for a few minutes about certain phases of this entire concept of what part men have in teaching us the Word in relation to the Spirit's ministry. To do this I need to discuss briefly with you four matters which may at first appear to be unrelated.

The first is the inductive method of Bible study. I want to say at the outset that the inductive method of Bible study is a good method, but it is one method among others, and no one has proved to my satisfaction at least that it is necessarily the best method. But it is a good method, and you ought to study the Bible inductively at times. This means that you simply see what the Bible has to say on a given subject, and you derive your doctrine or conclusions from your careful examination of all the verses that relate to that particular subject. One of the most fruitful uses of the inductive method is to take a concordance and trace all the uses of a word through the Bible, and then tie up the conclusions in a neat package. You will get some very excellent sermons from this kind of study of the Bible.

Suppose, for instance, you want to find out all about the biblical doctrine of fear. You simply take a concordance and look up and study all the references to fear in the Bible. But if you are a freshman, you may come out with different conclusions from what a senior may conclude. Do you know why? Simply because the freshman is apt to use an abbreviated concordance like Cruden's while the senior is more likely to use a complete concordance like Young's or Strong's. And the senior will discover that in the New Testament alone there are three different words for fear, which, if not distinguished, will result in contradictory conclusions. For example, in 2 Timothy 1:7 we are told we do not have a spirit of fear, while in 1 Peter 2:17 we are told to fear God. This contradiction can be solved only by referring to the two different Greek words used in these two verses. You see, even inductive study has to be done with skill and intelligence. To make good inductions you have to know both Greek and Hebrew or at least be able to read intelligently the books of those who do. So even the inductive approach includes the necessity of using the works of others under the guidance of the Holy Spirit.

Second, let's consider again the teaching ministry of the Spirit. I do not want to leave any impression that I am underestimating the importance of this ministry. But I do want to make it clear that the Spirit often teaches us through people—through books, through classes, through assignments, through exams, through term papers, and sometimes without apparently using any means. But please do not think because the Spirit of God has taught you something through another man that this something is any less important truth than if He had taught you without using a human teacher. Ultimately He does the teaching whether He chooses to use intermediaries or not.

Third, let's think a moment about our heritage. I simply mean this: If the Lord didn't want you to use any books or learn from men or study commentaries, then you should have been born in the first century. But the simple fact that you were born in the twentieth century gives you a rich heritage. You stand today as an heir of all the thought and labor of the many worthies of Church history who then - selves have given their lifetimes to the study of the Word. Just think of it—in the relatively short space of a few hours or a few days you can read what may have taken many years for someone to produce. You can read, for instance, all those wonderful volumes which took Calvin his whole lifetime to write in a lot less time than that. You do not have to wish you had lived in that former day when you could have heard the great Spurgeon preach. You can drop by the library anytime and hear him again through his books. Learn to read even things that are not assigned! This is part of your rich inheritance in things pertaining to the knowledge of God.

Fourth, I want to cite the example of Paul (2 Tim 4:13). Here is man about to be beheaded, and he knew it. Here is a man in prison at the end of his life. Now, when you come to any time of crisis, and particularly to the end of your life, you begin to see very clearly what is important and what is not. Paul reveals in this verse what he wanted during these last days of his life on earth. He wanted his cloak to keep him warm in the dungeon, his books, which were his commentaries on the Bible, and his parchments, which were probably copies of portions of the Old Testament which he was privileged to own. Imagine, calling for his books when he knew he did not have long to live. There are many interesting ramifications of this. Let me mention a few. Why in the world would any man facing death want to study? Or why should a man who had received direct revelations from God on several occasions need to read what mere men wrote? Why should one who was used by the Spirit of God to convey God's inspired message in writing be interested in the uninspired writings of men? Or why should a missionary be bothered carting his books around? Paul evidently valued his inheritance in books. Do you?

Finally, two conclusions from all that I have said. The first is this: You may be thinking this chapter has little application to you because obviously you are studying what other men have taught. But someday you will graduate, I hope, and then you will be on your own. No one will tell you that you have to read so many pages of collateral reading.

There will be no assignments. What will you do then? Will you coast along on "the Lord gave me this this morning"? Or will you continue studying so the Lord can really give you something accurate those mornings?

The second is this: If books are important, then what are you doing about accumulating some right now? I know what you are immediately thinking—you do not have any money. But you do have money for other things that are not absolute necessities, and you always have money for things you think are important. By the time you graduate, you ought to have the beginnings of a helpful library. If it is important to be taught by the Spirit through the works of other men, then it is important to be buying books today. Do not say you do not need anyone to teach you the Bible. You do. I hope you are taking full advantage of all the means God has put at your disposal to learn the Bible.

# 15

## *"I Don't Want Anyone to See Me, Just the Lord"*

THE LAST PIOUS FRAUD I want you to think about is a very tricky one. I had a great deal of difficulty giving it a title. Even in the title I have chosen, you will see a lot of truth, for it is a noble goal in the Christian life to want people to see only Christ in your life and not to see you. The living Christ should be seen in every believer's life, and it should be your godly ambition that people see the Lord, not you. But when the statement is reversed—"I don't want anyone to see me, just the Lord"—it sometimes becomes an excuse and is used as a cover-up for carelessness or sin. It is implied that if the Lord is being seen in any way at all, then it doesn't make much difference what I do, because, after all, I have told you not to look at me, just the Lord. Then, of course, it follows that you must not criticize me, because I've already explained that you are not supposed to look at me anyway. In other words, I am using this title as a statement of a fraud to cover up and excuse things which are either wrong, lacking, or improper in my life.

Naturally, there is scriptural support for the true aspect of the fraud. Many of you have already thought of Philippians 1:21: "For to me to live is Christ." Others are thinking Galatians 2:20: "I am crucified with Christ: nevertheless I live; yet not I, but Christ liveth in me: and the life which I now live in the flesh I live by the faith of the Son of God, who loved me, and gave himself for me." Perhaps you have in mind 1 Peter 2:21: "That ye should follow his steps." Or you might be thinking of Acts 4:13: "Now when they saw the boldness of Peter and John, and perceived that they were unlearned and ignorant men, they marvelled; and they took knowledge of them, that they had been with Jesus." Or perhaps a freshman (certainly not a senior!) is recalling that verse in the transfiguration story which says, "And when they had lifted up their eyes, they saw no man, save Jesus only" (Matt 17:8). Of course, many of these Scriptures are relevant and do support the truth that Christ should be seen in a believer's life. But twisting the truth into a fraud and the results of such perversion concern me greatly.

The inevitable result of this pious fraud is false humility. True humility is enjoined in the Scriptures, but there is nothing worse than false humility. Christian humility is God-consciousness. I am humble when I am conscious of God and live like it. This does not mean that I am humble because I have ceased to do anything, be anything, or say anything. But some people have the idea that humility is proved by one's becoming a nonentity. Quite the contrary, in humility I am conscious of the entity God has made me through Christ, of His power, and of His purposes for me. This does not necessarily mean that I am always talking about God, though obviously it means that many times I

97

do. It means primarily that I live in full cognizance of my relationship to Him in Christ.

If you have ever been in the presence of a person whom you know to be very wealthy, I doubt that you heard that person talk incessantly about his wealth. But you knew from his every action, from his bearing, from his topics of conversation, from his attitudes, that he was wealthy. Truly wealthy people are humble about it in the proper sense. It is only the people who think they are wealthy, or who are newly rich, who let you know about it. Similarly, when you are in the presence of a God-conscious person—one who is wealthy in spiritual things—he lets you know about it by his interest, his conversation, his bearing, his attitudes. Doing nothing is a false kind of humility, and often the person who piously has to say that he doesn't want you to see him, just the Lord, is the very one who is not doing anything.

One of the ways this fraud is used is to cover up poor preaching. Have you ever come from a preaching service where the message was poor, the homiletics worse, the grammar bad, but where there were some results from the preacher's pulpit-pounding and yelling? And have you ever had someone remark about how wonderful the service was? Well, you scarcely know what to say in such a situation. Since the preacher "really preached" with his pounding and yelling, that is supposed to excuse his poor homiletics and grammar. Even the evident blessing of the Lord on His Word is supposed to excuse the man's mistakes, because, after all, we don't look at the man anyway. Do not make any mistake about it—God is not pleased with your poor homiletics, lack of preparation, bad grammar, or offensive manner. It doesn't make any difference whether or not you "really preached"; you did not serve the Lord acceptably if you used bad grammar and these other things. Christ is not seen in sloppy preparation, poor presentation, and misuse of the English language. Every message you preach should not only be well thought out, but it also ought to be gift wrapped in the most attractive kind of package. You need to have the Lord's message, to be sure; but you also need to present it in an appealing way. But sometimes this fraud—"Don't look at me, just see the Lord"—is used as a cover-up for lack of proper presentation and preparation on the part of the messenger.

Sometimes the fraud is used to justify a change in the message. You know what I mean. "I was going to preach on such and such a subject today, but the Lord changed my mind." Now the Lord does do this sometimes; but when He does, be sure that He changes your mind from one prepared message to another prepared message. And be sure the change of mind is not because you happened to spot so-and-so in the the audience who you think needs to hear the other message. There might be six people whose lives you do not know about who needed that first message.

Sometimes the fraud is used to justify a change of invitation. In my mind there is nothing more dishonest than to give one invitation which guarantees no further invitation and then say that the Lord has led you to give a further invitation. You tell people that all you are going to ask them to do is raise their hands, and then, after you finally get a few hands raised, you say the Lord has led you to ask them to come forward. I do not see the Lord in this; all I see is a dishonest invitation.

Or sometimes this fraud is used to excuse a student's

studying on the job. Not long ago a man who employs a student was complaining to me that the student was studying on the job. After he assured me that the person had been told not to do so, I advised him to warn the student and if the studying persisted to fire him. But he was reluctant to do this simply because the student was studying the Bible on the job. You see, a pious fraud was being used to cheat an honest employer.

Let's go back to some of these verses which I said are sometimes used to support this idea. I want to try to help you see them in their proper perspective.

I assume I do not need to say anything about Matthew 17:8. When the disciples "saw no man, save Jesus only" that was exactly what they saw on that historic occasion of the transfiguration. It has no relevance to the present subject.

The notice of the Jewish religious leaders that Peter and John had been with Jesus means two things (Acts 4:13). First, it means they recognized that these disciples, like their Master, were intelligent men, though they had not been trained formally in the rabbinic schools. "Unlearned and ignorant" in that verse means untrained in the schools, not unintelligent. Second, it means that, like Jesus, the disciples spoke with authority.

But it is Philippians 1:21 and Galatians 2:20 that are more pertinent. Just what does "to me to live is Christ" mean? It means "to me, living is Christ." "From my viewpoint," Paul is saying, "living is Christ." Doubtless the power of the Christian life, the indwelling Christ, is included in what he is saying. But he also means that his purpose, his interest, his outlook, his activities, his goal in living is Christ. "To me," he declares, "living—its power,

100

interests, ambitions, everything about living—is Christ."
Living is not something that is dead ; it is something very
much alive because it is centered in Christ. It means living
for Him, and it means living to reflect Him.

But what about Galatians 2:20? I want to point out
something in this verse which you may have overlooked.
Usually you hear the verse quoted to emphasize the fact
that it is only Christ living in us that enables us to live at all.
It's the *Christ*-living-in-me emphasis that is heard. The
human personality is deemphasized, if not completely
erased, so that, we are told, all we need is to have Christ
live His life through us. Let me read the verse, emphasizing
different words. "*I* am crucified with Christ: nevertheless *I*
live; yet not *I*, but Christ liveth in *me:* and the life which *I*
now live in the *flesh I* live by the faith of the Son of God,
who loved *me*, and gave himself for *me*." There are more
references in this verse to *me* than there are to Christ. Far
from toning down the human personality, the verse em-
phasizes it. Let's examine it further. "I am crucified with
Christ." This does not mean I cease to exist. Crucifixion
means death, and death in the Scriptures never means
cessation of existence. It always means separation. My
cocrucifixion with Christ means my separation from the
power of sin. He died unto sin once, and I died with Him.
When Paul declares that the Christian has been crucified
with Christ, he means he has been separated from bad
homiletics, from laziness in studies, from breaking school
rules, from bad grammar, from everything displeasing to
God. When you quote Galatians 2:20, be sure you understand the full impact of all you are claiming.

But we are not left in a state of negative separation. We
have also been raised to a new life. It's the life which Christ

101

lives through me, but please note that He is living it through *me*. *I* live, Paul says. I haven't ceased to be, but I am a new I, and it is I who have been changed. Now I have new ambitions, new desires, new discipline, new outlooks, new attitudes, new conversation. But *I* am the one living. A new I to be sure but not an obliterated I. Therefore, what I do is important, and people around will see Christ through me, not apart from me. So, you see, you can't say, "Don't look at me, just Christ," because I can't look at Christ without looking at you. And if I see or hear things which are not Christlike, then I have been blinded to seeing Him.

Let me quote another New Testament verse which places what I have been trying to say in perfect balance. It is Matthew 5:16: "Let your light so shine before men, that they may see your good works, and glorify your Father which is in heaven." You are the way men see Christ. Your speech, your grammar, your actions at work, your discipline, your courteousness are all important. I cannot see the Lord except through you. And when something is out of joint in your life, please do not try to cover it up by saying, however piously, "I don't want you to see me, just the Lord." The statement is true in that I am supposed to see the Lord in you, but it is also true that this comes about by seeing in you an upright, honest, intelligent person. This is something that does not happen in a single meeting; it takes a lifetime of development. But it begins now.

# 16

## *Three R's*

EVERY CHRISTIAN is in a race, and young people have the happy privilege of having most of it yet ahead of them. Here are three R's to help you be a winner in the race of the Christian life.

The first *R* stands, as you would suspect, for the race. The ancient Greeks and the people of New Testament times whom they influenced loved their athletic contests. We're all familiar with the Olympic Games, but Olympia was just one city in which games were held, and there were stadia in other cities of the Hellenistic world. So it is not surprising that sports, which are so much a vital part of young people's lives, are often used in the New Testament to illustrate the Christian life.

I walked once among the ruins of ancient Ephesus and saw the remains of the old stadium in that city. It was the same stadium which Paul himself saw when he lived there. From Ephesus he wrote these words to the Corinthians and to us:

> Know ye not that they which run in a race run all, but one receiveth the prize? So run, that ye may obtain. And every

man that striveth for the mastery is temperate in all things. Now they do it to obtain a corruptible crown; but we an incorruptible. I therefore so run, not as uncertainly; so fight I, not as one that beateth the air: but I keep under my body, and bring it into subjection: lest that by any means, when I have preached to others, I myself should be a castaway [Gk., "disapproved"] (1 Cor 9:24-27).

Will you notice two things about this race? First of all, it covers a definite distance. In Paul's day it was two hundred yards, but in relation to the Christian life it is an illustration of that definite, detailed, and distinctive plan which the Lord Jesus Christ has worked out for each one of you. It's a wonderful thing to know He has such a plan for your life, and it ought to make you want to be definite in your planning as well. I don't believe any one of you is too young to be thinking about these things, for the matter of who is going to direct your life is a very basic one. If God runs your life, you'll win the race; if you run it, you'll lose.

Second, the race is a demanding one. The competition is stiff because, for you as a Christian running the race of the Christian life, your opponents are the world with all its attractions, the flesh within you, and Satan who tries his hardest to counterfeit God's plan for your life. When the competition is stiff, you have to play the harder. You see, the Christian life is not for sissies; it takes a real man or woman to win this race. Also, when the competition is stiff, your strategy has to be planned more carefully. You have to be alert to everything that is going on around you and use your every faculty to the fullest.

The second R stands for the rules of this race. The thought of rules is not a pleasant one for young people, but rules are not only necessary—they are actually beneficial, if you want to be a winner. Aren't you glad dairy companies have rules about the purity of their products? Aren't traffic laws beneficial in keeping us all from being killed? Even rules about assignments are a help, for they keep you from flunking! Every sport has its rules, and no player can be a winner without keeping them. The Christian life is no exception. If you want to be a winner, you must live the life according to God's rules. Paul said in another place, "And if a man also strive for masteries, yet is he not crowned, except he strive lawfully" (2 Tim 2:5).

Many principles in the Bible concern living the Christian life, but just three are mentioned in this text. First, "every man that striveth for the mastery is temperate in all things"; that is, condition your body. This means a vigorous, active, self-control of your body so you'll be physically fit to do any kind of service for the Lord. Not only do those hard places of the earth demand top physical condition, but every aspect of the Lord's work requires the best of you. There's no better time to be conditioning your bodies than right now. Greek athletes trained under oath for ten months before a race. Christians should do that and more for their Lord.

The second rule can be stated like this: Control your body; that is, have a goal in life. Be asking the Lord now what He would have you do with your life, and then aim everything—the subjects you take, the extracurricular activities, the college you choose—toward this purpose. Paul uses two illustrations in the passage to emphasize this. He says, "Don't be like a runner who runs uncertainly— perhaps in the wrong direction or halfheartedly." "Neither," he adds, "be like a shadow boxer who is always swinging and never hitting anything." Have you got an aim in life? That's what it means to control your body.

The third rule is found in the words "I keep under my body [literally, beat it black-and-blue], and bring it into subjection"; that is, capture your body. You must be the master of your body to use it under God's direction for carrying out His purpose for your life. You should be physically fit, and that fitness must be a means to the end of serving God and never an end in itself.

In summary, the rules are simply these: Build your body into the very best condition possible; then aim your life toward His goal for you; and let your conditioned body be controlled by the Lord for His purposes. These are the principles which you must follow to be a winner in the race.

The third *R* is for reward. When the race is over, every participant (which means every Christian) will stand before the Lord Jesus to be judged for the kind of Christian life lived. Useless works will be burned, and rewards will be given for good works. Paul wrote, "So run, that ye may obtain." Run as if there were going to be only one winner and you are going to be that man. Anything that will hinder you should be shunned; everything that helps must be used.

If you are a Christian, you are automatically in the race. But let me ask you, What kind of a race are you running? Is is according to God's rules or your own? Do you want God's will for your life? Are you trying to be a winner? Will the Lord be able to look over your life and say, "Well run"? "One receiveth the prize. So run, that ye may obtain."

# 17

## *On the QT*

SOME OF YOU KNOW I have written several booklets of object lessons. The first one was published during my first year of teaching, and I used to get a lot of kidding from my students about it. Instead of calling it by its right title, *Easy Object Lessons,* they dubbed it "This Is an Onion Series." Now the reason for this rather undignified title was simply that there was one lesson in the booklet that used an onion as the object. It went something like this. I would rub the onion over my hand, put the onion out of sight, then have someone smell my hand and ask if he could tell where my hand had been. Of course, it was always pretty obvious that my hand had been next to an onion. The point of this easy object lesson is simply that it is just as easy to tell where a Christian has been—whether he has been with the Lord or with the world.

You know, this can be illustrated by many experiences of life. When one of you girls has just come from the beauty parlor you don't have to hang a sign around your neck advertising the fact. We all know it by just looking at you.

Even when you fellows are getting ready to go out on a date we can tell it. As they say—you sure smell pretty. And it's not because you're going to the dining room to eat by yourself.

When you have been with the Lord, people can tell it easily. And when you flirt with the world, the same is true. The time you spend with the Lord will always show in your life, and I want to talk to you about that quiet time which every Christian should have.

First of all I want to remind you why you need a quiet time. You remember that Christ Himself set the example. Mark tells us, "And in the morning, rising up a great while before day, he went out, and departed into a solitary place, and there prayed" (1:35). It is as true as it is obvious that if Christ needed to be alone with His Father, certainly we do too.

Time alone with the Lord is necessary not only because we need help personally but because others need the help we can give them in prayer. During the quiet time you can enjoy the privilege of exercising your ministry as a priest of God in helping other people.

But you also need time alone with the Lord in order to get to know Him better. Of course, you can get to know the Lord in many ways and through many experiences of life. But there is a distinct and particular way that you come to know Him in the quiet time that you cannot experience by any other means.

Let me illustrate. Some people get married on a shoe-string. My wife and I got married on a schedule. We had hardly returned from a short honeymoon when we were off to a series of summer Bible conferences. Now, the program of Bible conferences is always full, and it doesn't leave much time to get acquainted with your wife, especially when you're the speaker. But this was the way it was during the first few months of our marriage. Finally, one night we happened to have an evening alone. There was no meeting scheduled, and nothing pressing. My wife and I were sitting talking when suddenly she said to me, "Isn't it nice just to have time to talk to each other?" And it was, for it gave us some time just to get to know each other's hopes, plans, ambitions, and desires—time which we hadn't had in the busy schedule of Bible conferences.

Now, you can get to know the Lord in the classroom, or while teaching a Sunday school class, or at a street meeting, or in the many other activities to which you are wedded here in school, but there is a distinct, unique, and absolutely necessary way by which you must come to know your Lord that is achieved only in your quiet time.

These are the reasons for quiet time: because Christ set the example, because others need help, and because you need that intimate acquaintance with the Lord that comes only during that time. Of course, if you don't see any reason for having a personal time with the Lord, then that indicates that Christ's example means little or nothing to you, that the need of others is of little or no concern to you, and that you don't really want to know better the Lord who saved you.

But I think deep down all of you realize the importance of a quiet time. We sense the need, but we do not know exactly how to go about having an effective quiet time.

Let me say something, then, about the nature of a good quiet time with the Lord Jesus. The most important rule about any quiet time is to do what is best for you personally. I am always reluctant to set down rules, because it is impossible to say what would be best for hundreds of people. I might be able to devise a set of rules for two or three, but not for all. That is why the overall governing principle ought to be: do whatever is best for you. Having a quiet time is somewhat like baking a cake. In every cake there are certain basic ingredients. In every quiet time there have to be certain basic things, too. But as there are also different kinds of cake that you can make from these basic ingredients by adding other different ingredients, there are also different ways you can enjoy your own quiet time. Some people like chocolate cake, and others like white cake. The particular form which your own quiet time may take may not be quite the same as someone else's, but there will be certain basic ingredients in all of our quiet times, and it is only of these basics that I wish to speak.

The first and most important one is regularity. It is far more important for you to spend five minutes each day with the Lord than one hour once a week. It is far more important for you to do something regularly than to do nothing for a while, and then do a lot, and then nothing. If you are not yet to the place in your Christian life where you have five minutes a day with the Lord, then by all means do that much regularly before you try to do more. As you grow in the Lord you will want to spend more time, but do not bite off more than you can chew right now. Do not start off with a resolution to spend a lot of time in your devotions and then find yourself failing the second or third day. Failure will discourage you and cause you to lapse into irregularity. Resolve to do only that which you honestly feel you can do every day, and you will be more apt to stick to it.

The time of the day when you have your quiet time is not

even so important as this matter of regularity. Some of you find morning the best; others prefer evening. You know your own physical makeup and your schedule, and I cannot tell you which time is best for you. If you just cannot wake up in the morning and you are wide awake at night, then you had better use the evening; only be sure you start early enough so you do not fall asleep while you are praying. If you are the kind who falls asleep while undressing, then be sure you spend time with the Lord in the morning. The important thing is to do it and do it regularly.

It might even be a good idea to do something both morning and evening. At least pray briefly before you begin your day. Remember what the psalmist said: "My voice shalt thou hear in the morning, O LORD; in the morning will I direct my prayer unto thee, and will look up" (Psalm 5:3). Remember, too, that we are told by Paul not to let the sun go down on our wrath (Eph 4:26). These verses seem to indicate a need in the morning for prayer to prepare us for the day, and a need in the evening for cleaning off the sins that have accumulated during the course of that day. If you have a roommate you might like to share one prayer time with him and have the other alone.

There is a second ingredient which must be in everybody's quiet time. It is the Bible, for this is the way God speaks to you. If you are having difficulty in maintaining an interest in God's Word, may I suggest you try reading in several places in the Bible until you find some part that especially interests you. There is no rule that says you have to start with Genesis or John. Start where you like; only, if you are trying to find out if a certain book interests you, be sure to give it a fair trial. Read in it for three days at least.

Then if you do not find it **particularly** interesting, read somewhere else for three days. The point is, read, and read consistently in some place. God speaks to you in His Word, so you will have to read it in order to hear Him.

With your reading there should be thinking. I was going to use the word *meditation*, but for some people meditation is the same as daydreaming. What I mean is that you should think unhurriedly about what you are reading. At the same time it is necessary to keep going and not lapse into daydreaming. Perhaps the word *application* better conveys what I have in mind. Think about what you are reading, not in some far-off way, but as it relates to you yourself. Apply to your own life what God is saying to you each day through His Word. Some days you may want to read a lengthy portion. Other days you may want to concentrate on a shorter passage. Sometimes you may want to spend the time memorizing some verse. But let God speak to you in the long portion, the short portion, or the single memory verse.

The third ingredient is prayer. I have already quoted verses which show we should pray in the morning and in the evening. Never go to bed with some disagreement or difficulty that has not been cleared up. If you get hurt or griped during the course of a day, just be sure you do not go to sleep with that thing on your heart. Prayer is necessary for a lot of reasons—confession, praise, problems, requests, strength, wisdom. In the morning pray through the activities of the day. Pray for each class, every teacher, chapel, for your home pastor, for missionaries you know. There is so much to pray for that no one should ever wonder what he can say to the Lord. If it helps you to keep a list, then do so; only be sure you keep it up-to-date. If it is a long list do not try to pray through the entire list every day. Divide it up. Whatever helps you use, be sure they are means to the end and not ends in themselves.

Now, in addition to all these ingredients—regularity, the Word, prayer—there must be one other, discipline. We all face two problems in this matter of discipline. The first is the problem of pressure. But let me tell you something—if you think you are under pressure now, wait until you get out of school. But pressures are solved by priorities. Learn now to decide what is important and what is secondary. Is it more important to have time with the Lord either in the morning or at night than to have an extra hour talking to someone or just plain messing around? If you think it is important to be with the Lord, you will get to bed at a decent hour and there will not be any pressure on you in the morning when you ought to get up. The pressures of schedules and busyness will all be solved by the principle of priorities.

The second problem we all face is that of procrastination. We are all, I suppose, procrastinators by nature, and this natural inclination is aided and abetted by the devil, who does his very best to keep us from having our quiet time with the Lord. The only solution I know for this problem of procrastination is persistence. Stick with it. Be persistent, and ask the Lord to especially help in this problem.

How is your devotional life with the Lord? Perhaps you once started out well, but as the weeks went on you have become irregular in this matter. Maybe you have excused yourself by saying you are not getting out of your quiet time what you feel you should. Do not rely on feelings. Your job

**113**

is to stick to it. How has it been this week? And what are you going to do about it? Start today, not tomorrow, and start doing something, and stick with it.

# 18

## *Why Not Pray?*

SINCE PRAYER is one of the basic ingredients in every successful quiet time, I want to pursue the matter a little further. I am sure none of us would debate the importance of the subject; and I am inclined to think there is too much talking about prayer and too little doing of it. But sometimes talk helps. And even though many of the things I say may be familiar to some of you, I hope just thinking about these things will be of some help.

I want to ask and answer two questions today: first, Why don't we pray? and second, Why should we pray?

First of all, I want you to think about some of the reasons why we do not pray as we should. There are many reasons one could give, but I want to stick to three. The first is something we are seldom conscious of. It does not often affect us consciously; nevertheless, it does affect all of us at some time or another. It is this: We do not pray as we ought simply because we cannot see God. "God is a Spirit: and they that worship him must worship him in spirit and in truth" (John 4:24). Whether we realize it or not, it is hard to communicate with someone we cannot see. There is, con-

115

sciously or unconsciously, a barrier raised. In many instances it becomes more difficult to pray to our heavenly Father just because we cannot see Him.

Perhaps I can illustrate what I mean by telling you about the first time I preached on the radio. We were broadcasting not from a studio but from a lounge, and there were present in the room besides myself just a pianist, a vocalist, an announcer, and the engineer. This was supposed to be an evangelistic message, and when I got up to speak, I was suddenly floored. I looked at the engineer. He was not paying any attention to me, which was right, since he had other far more important things to do. Then I looked at the pianist. He was flipping the pages of the hymnbook looking for the closing hymn. I looked at the soloist. He was making sign language at the pianist. Only the announcer was listening to me. He was also a theological student, as I was, and I knew full well that he had no need of an evangelistic message. And that did not help my attitude at all. None of the people I could see needed to hear what I was about to say, and since I could not see the hundreds of people who were listening and who did need the Gospel, I thought, *What's the use of even preaching this message?* If I could have realized how many invisible people there were listening to me at the moment, I would not have been so frustrated.

This is something like the problem we consciously or unconsciously face when we pray. It is simply not easy to talk to someone we cannot see.

How can we help overcome this problem? By simply remembering that the Lord Jesus Christ was the visible expression of the Father. By this I do not mean that we should try to imagine what Christ's face looks like when we pray, but I do mean that we should try to come to know what Christ's character is like so we can know what God's character is like. If you know something about a person, you feel you know the person even though you may never have met him. And knowing the facts about the life and ministry of Christ will help you to know what He is like, and this will help overcome whatever problem may be involved in God's being invisible. It is not a picture of Christ or God we need in order to be able to pray better, but we do need to know His character better through His Word.

There's a second reason why many of us do not pray. It is simply that we are embarrassed. Of course, this has to do more with praying in public than in private. The remedy for this problem is simply, *do it!* Make yourself get up and pray in a prayer meeting. Start in some small group where you will be apt to be least embarrassed. Remember, too, that there is one good rule to follow—short prayers in public, long prayers in private. Most people reverse the rule, and you cannot help but wonder if they ever pray privately since they seem to spend most of their public praying time catching up on what they should have been doing in private. When you lead in public prayer, remember you are leading everybody in the group; so make it short and to the point.

A third reason why we do not pray—and this is one that applies to all of us—is that we do not have enough time. This is a genuine problem, and I do not minimize it. We are all pressed for time, and we are all busy. We all have schedules and deadlines to meet, and, as a result, prayer time gets crowded out of our day. To meet this problem may I suggest two things. First, ask the Lord to show you how important prayer is. We all can find time for that which we consider important, and if you realize how much priority God gives to this matter of praying, you will find time to do it yourself. Second, make yourself form the habit of praying now. I repeat, it is more important to pray five minutes every day than it is to pray one hour once a week. The five minutes will become an established habit in your life, and soon it will increase to more than five minutes. Of course, this is not something that will happen overnight. Habits are not formed in twenty-four hours. This is something that needs to be cultivated, encouraged, fought with, and prayed about in order to begin to cultivate the habit of regular praying. The time to start is *now*, not tomorrow.

Do you remember Daniel? He formed the habit of praying three times a day early in his life, and when the king had signed the decree which would put him in the lions' den, Daniel did not have to run suddenly to the Lord and frantically try to learn how to pray. He knew how to pray because he had been doing it for seventy years or more.

Now the second question I want to ask and answer is this: Why should we pray? We do not pray because it is hard to pray to an unseen person, because in public we sometimes tend to be embarrassed, and because we all have the problem of finding time. But we know we should pray, and perhaps just reviewing some of the reasons why we should will help remind us of the importance of prayer.

The first reason why we should pray is that God commands it. There are many passages in the Bible that speak of it, but I will only remind you of three. The first is Luke 18:1: "Men ought always to pray, and not to faint." That word *faint* means "become disheartened or weary." Men ought always to pray and not become disheartened or grow weary. The second is Colossians 4:2: "Continue in prayer, and watch in the same with thanksgiving." The third is 1 Thessalonians 5:17: "Pray without ceasing."

These are familiar verses, but I was interested to find that each one has a slightly different emphasis. The word *always* used in Luke 18:1 is the usual word in the New Testament for always and means "in every situation and circumstance."

In Colossians 4:2 the verb *continue* is a compound verb built on a root which means "strength." In other words, to continue in prayer means to "give strength" to your praying. Or we might say "be devoted to prayer," or "give your energy to prayer." The idea is that we are to be energetic in prayer.

In 1 Thessalonians 5:17 we are told to pray without ceasing. This term "without ceasing" is used of having a hacking cough. Now, when you have a hacking cough you are not actually coughing all the time, even though the cough is always there. If you had such a chronic coughing condition, it would be described in Greek by this term "without ceasing." This is the meaning of praying without ceasing. The meaning is not that every waking moment shall be spent in actual praying, but it does mean that every moment should be prayerful. And this prayerful attitude will erupt into actual prayer many times during the course of a day.

The second reason why we should pray is that we need to. But we all have excuses. One is that God is too great to be interested in us and our needs. We can never reach Him because He is too great. It is true that a great person cannot be personally interested in everything and everybody under him. People are limited. But God has another quality besides greatness, and that is infinity. He is not only

119

great but infinite, thus He can always be interested in you personally and individually.

But the second excuse is one I hear more frequently. "Why pray? What's going to happen is going to happen anyway." This is simply fatalism. Let me tell you something. It is not going to happen *any* way; it is going to happen a *certain* way, and that certain way is in answer to your prayers.

The day of Pentecost is a good example of this. It was going to happen because it had been prophesied. It was absolutely certain that Pentecost would come. The Old Testament had foreshadowed it, and the Lord Jesus had given the disciples a definite promise of it (Acts 1:5). What did the disciples do? Did they take ten days off and have a big time? Why should they not have? After all, the promise was sure. No, they prayed, and their involvement in prayer was a necessary part of God's fulfillment of the promise of Pentecost. Things are not going to happen *any* way. They are going to happen *through your praying*. And that is why you need to pray.

The third reason why we should pray is this: God needs our fellowship in prayer. We do not believe in a deistic concept of God which says that although He started everything He now has no interest in His creation. God does desire our fellowship in prayer.

Suppose I should announce to you today that I had just made arrangements to move into a students' dormitory. You would be astonished and would say, "What about your wife and family?" Well, I intend to take care of them. I am going to continue to pay the bills. They will go on living at home. I will buy the groceries. I will even do the shopping. But I am going to move into a dorm. You would say:

"You are crazy." And I think you would be right. I could insist to you over and over that I love them, but you would not believe me if I were living in a dorm without them. And you can tell me that you love the Lord, but I have trouble believing you unless you spend time with Him in prayer. You need it, and He needs it, just as I need my family and they need me. If you really love Him, you will spend time in fellowship with Him.

These are some of the reasons why we do not, and why we should, pray. I hope they have been of some help, and that each of you will learn to enjoy praying much during all the years God lets you live.

# 19

## *How Do I Pray?*

I want to answer the question, How are we supposed to pray? How can we be sure God hears us when we pray—to say nothing of how to be sure our prayers can be answered. I am going to present three propositions—two negative and one positive—that will answer this question.

The first is this: Correct praying does not necessarily involve a certain time. Some people think it does. You must pray in the morning, they imply, or you will not be heard. Well, the Bible does give us examples of praying in the morning (Mark 1:35), but it also gives examples of praying at night (Luke 6:12). Further, there are examples of praying at mealtimes (Acts 27:35; 1 Tim 4:4-5) and even at set times during the day (Acts 2:46; 3:1; 10:9, 30). As a matter of fact, you will remember that we are told to pray always (Eph 6:18). So time is not the important consideration in how to pray.

The second is this: Correct praying is not necessarily dependent upon a certain posture. It is positively amazing, when you look through the Bible, to discover that people prayed in almost every conceivable position. They prayed standing (Gen 18:22); kneeling (Luke 22:41); with face on the ground (Matt 26:39); with head between the knees (1 Kings 18:42); seated (2 Sam 7:18); in bed (Psalm 63:6); on land (John 17:1); on the sea (Matt 14:30); and even in the air (Luke 23:42). In other words, any posture has scriptural warrant as long as you keep awake and alert. Now, of course I do not recommend that you pray lying in bed if you are the kind of person who is out like a light as soon as his head hits the pillow; but if you are an insomniac, then bed would be a very useful place for lots of praying. I suggest you use the position that keeps you most alert when you pray.

So you see, it is not the time or the posture that guarantees answers to prayer. Correct praying is—and this is the third proposition—praying in His name. The Lord Jesus could not have put it more simply when He said, "If ye shall ask any thing in my name, I will do it (John 14:14).

I am sure you have read or heard messages on praying in the name of Christ, so I wanted to try to find some approach which would give you a different slant or a fresh view of what it means. I thought the best way I could do this would be to use an illustration, develop it, and examine some of its particulars. The illustration is not a common one, but I am sure you will understand it readily.

When I went abroad to study, I discovered that one did not just buy a ticket and step aboard a ship or plane. There are a lot of preparations that have to be made. Not only are there shots, passport, and visas, but you also have to see to it that your affairs at home will be attended to while you are out of the country. For one thing, you have to make arrangements to get money somehow, since there is no place in this world where you can live without it. If you own property, you have to see to it that someone looks after it to pay the taxes, collect the rent, and take care of things generally. All the things you normally do when you are at home still have to be done when you are away. Well, to facilitate matters in my own case, I signed a document called a power of attorney.

It was a very long document which gave my father the right and power to do anything in my name. Of course, a power of attorney can be appointed for a specific thing. Many people set up their checking accounts at banks with a power of attorney to their husbands or wives so that someone will be empowered to sign checks for them in case of illness or accident. But in my case I made an **all-inclusive** power of attorney so that whatever came up in **my absence** could be cared for in my name. I must confess, **however,** that when I read the document I was rather startled to see exactly what power I was turning over to someone else, even though that someone was my father. He could borrow money in my name, and of course I would have been liable for the debt; he could have sold **any property** I might have owned; he could have played **the stock** market in my name, and I would have been **responsible** for all the losses; he could have taken a fancy vacation and signed the checks in my name. I had given him blanket power, but I had not given him a blank check, for I knew my father would never do anything of which I would not approve. It was blanket power, but he would only use it in ways that would meet my approval.

When our Lord Jesus went back to heaven He gave to you and me as His attornies this kind of power—power to ask what He would want us to ask in His name. I want to suggest five things that are included in this.

The first is this: There is a relationship involved. You do not give just anybody the power of attorney. You give it to someone you know—either someone in your family or a trusted lawyer. Just so, God has entrusted us with this blanket power simply because we are His children. Of course, if there happens to be a black sheep in your family, you certainly would not make that relative your attorney. God expects us to use the power He has given us as faithful children, not black sheep.

The second thing involved is knowledge. I have deliberately chosen knowledge rather than faith because it is more basic, since faith is based on knowledge and increases as knowledge increases. The Lord said we could ask whatever we want *if* His words abide in us (John 15:7). Again, this is not a blank check. This is asking in His name on the basis of what we know about Him. If my father had been faced with a decision to make in my name while I was abroad, he would have asked himself, "What would Charles want?" and "What would be best?" When you kneel down to use the power of attorney God has given you, you will ask, "What does God want in this situation?" and "What would be best for God's interests?" Asking in His name involves knowledge—knowledge of Him as found in His Word.

The third thing involved is honesty. When you choose someone to handle your affairs, you obviously want someone who is thoroughly competent and honest, someone who is concerned for your interests and not for his own selfish interests. That is exactly what God wants when He asks us to pray for anything in His name. He wants us to be honest and to look out for His interests, not our own. It is so very easy to pray selfishly. For instance,

125

what motivated you in asking for the things you prayed about this morning? Why do you ask for a good grade on an exam? Why do you ask for a certain date? Whose interests do you have at heart, yours or God's? If they are not completely God's, then you are not asking in His name. You are not an honest attorney, because an honest one has only his client's interests at heart.

The fourth thing involved is work. When you give someone a power of attorney, you expect him to work for you. If there is a transaction to be completed, you expect him to be on the job and see that it is done. If there are forms to be filled out, he has to do it. If there are facts to be dug up, this is his responsibility. If there are errands to be run, he runs them because he is your attorney. You have hired him to do these things. God has given us the power to ask anything in His name. But this involves work. When you ask Him to bless missions and missionaries, this may mean you will have to be a missionary. When you ask Him to lead you, this will involve digging up some facts. When you ask Him for victory, it may mean working to form some good habits of holiness. You cannot ask in the name of the Lord unless you are also willing to be used in answering the very request that you are asking.

Finally, this relationship involves results. To ask in His name brings results. I would like to give you dozens of personal illustrations, but there is not time. Once when I was writing an important thesis, I was desperate for certain information to fill an important gap in my paper. I simply could not find any book that could help me or even any hint anywhere on that particular subject. One day I was just browsing in the stacks of the library, asking the Lord to help me find something, when my eye fell on a book that gave me exactly what I wanted. Even my professors did not know such a book existed.

I sincerely hope, young people, that you have many experiences of seeing your prayers, asked in His name, answered. Do not start with George Mueller's petitions. Start with your own needs in your own situation today. Ask about these things in His name intelligently, honestly, willingly, and you will see results.

## DATE DUE

'82